From
Birth to 5
Serving the Youngest
Handicapped Children

Roberta Weiner ■ Jane Koppelman

An Education Research Group Report

Capitol Publications, Inc.
1101 King Street, Alexandria, Virginia 22314

Also published by the Education Research Group:

The Child Abuse Crisis: Impact on the Schools
P.L. 94-142: Impact on the Schools
AIDS: Impact on the Schools
Teen Pregnancy: Impact on the Schools
Education Directory: A Guide to Decisionmakers in the Federal Government, the States and Education Associations
Inside the Education Department: An Office-by-Office Review
Education Regulations Library
The Education Evaluator's Workbook: How to Assess Education Programs
The Supreme Court and Education
Education Sourcebook: Where to Find the Materials You Need
The 1986 Tax Reform Act: Bad News for Nonprofits
Proven Plans for Recruiting and Retaining Students: 21 Case Studies

Copyright © 1987 by the Education Research Group, Capitol Publications, Inc.

Helen Hoart, Publisher
Roberta Weiner, Executive Editor

All rights reserved. No part of this book may be reproduced or used in any form without permission in writing from the publisher. Address inquiries to: Education Research Group, Capitol Publications, Inc., 1101 King St., Alexandria, Va. 22314.

Printed in the United States of America

Library of Congress Catalog Card Number 87-80171
ISBN 0-937925-21-7

Roberta Weiner, Jane Koppelman
 From Birth to Five: Serving the Youngest Handicapped Children

Cover design by Linda C. McDonald

First Edition

About The Authors

Roberta Weiner, executive editor of Capitol Publications' Education Research Group (ERG), has been an education writer and editor for eight years. Before taking the helm of ERG when it was formed in 1986, Ms. Weiner was managing editor of *Education Daily* and *Higher Education Daily*. She is also the author of *P.L. 94-142: Impact on the Schools* and *AIDS: Impact on the Schools*.

Ms. Weiner began her career at the *Middlesex News* in Framingham, Mass., where she was an education reporter. She has a bachelor of science degree in journalism from Boston University.

Jane Koppelman has been the editor of *Report on Preschool Programs,* a Capitol Publications newsletter that covers a variety of preschool and child care issues, since 1985. Prior to that, Ms. Koppelman edited *Handicapped Americans Report,* a newsletter on programs for handicapped adults. She is also the author of *Child Care Insurance Crisis: Strategies for Survival*.

Ms. Koppelman also has worked as an assistant producer for a variety of radio and television investigative news shows produced by the Canadian Broadcast Corporation. She has a bachelor of arts degree in broadcast journalism from the American University in Washington, D.C.

Table of Contents

	Page
Introduction	7

Chapter One
Overview	9
Why Now?	9
Costs	12
Phase-In Time	16
"A Small Miracle"	16

Chapter Two
Birth Through Two: Serving Handicapped Infants
And Toddlers	17
Selecting The Best Programs	18
Whom To Serve?	20
Existing Programs	24
Whose Job Is It?	28
Funding	30
Transition And Interagency Coordination	30
From Our Rolodex	33

Case Study 2.1
Adolescent-Infant Development Program, Washington, D.C.	35

Chapter Three
Three Through Five: Challenges In Serving Preschoolers	39
The Head Start Option	41
Turning The Tables On Integration	45
Public Possibilities	47
Funding Questions	49
From Our Rolodex	51

Case Study 3.1
Project STEPS, Lexington, Ky.	54

Case Study 3.2
High School/Preschool Partnership Program, Pinellas County, Fla.	59

Case Study 3.3
Early Childhood Education Program, Urbana, Ill.	64

Chapter Four
Personnel Preparation: Meeting The Demand	69
How Four States Deal With Shortages	70

Chapter Four (Cont.)
The Fine Line Of Certification 73
Serving Infants 76
Serving Rural Areas 81
Using Allied Health Professionals 82
From Our Rolodex 85
Case Study 4.1
Wheelock College Graduate School, Boston 86

Chapter Five
Child Care: The Family's Dilemma 89
Delaware 89
Pennsylvania 92
St. Louis, Missouri 92
Vermont 93
From Our Rolodex 94
Case Study 5.1
Extended Day Care Project, Madison, Wis. 95

Chapter Six
Parents: An Increasingly Powerful Role 99
Stages Of Grief 100
Monitoring And Education 101
From Our Rolodex 103
Case Study 6.1
Project Enlightenment, Raleigh, N.C. 104

Conclusion 109

Appendices

Appendix A
Text of P.L. 99-457 115

Appendix B
Minimum Age Mandates 156

Appendix C
Estimated Allocations, Fiscal 1987 161

Appendix D
Entry Level Skills Checklist 165

Appendix E
U.S. Office of Special Education Programs Directory 175

Appendix F
State Resource Directory 179

Bibliography 209

Introduction

Eleven years after the Education for All Handicapped Children Act, P.L. 94-142, challenged the nation's assumptions about educating handicapped children, Congress once again upset (in the best sense of the word) the status quo.

In the most sweeping set of changes to the Education of the Handicapped Act (EHA) since P.L. 94-142, Congress in fall 1986 added to EHA programs that put a new emphasis on children from birth through age 5. In short, today's focus is on serving the youngest, and, by virtue of their age, the most vulnerable handicapped children.

Early intervention is clearly the "top issue now" in special education, right up there with the ever-present dilemma over funding P.L. 94-142, said Frank New, state director of special education in Ohio and 1987-88 president of the National Association of State Directors of Special Education (NASDSE). It's the issue "most people are going to be spending large amounts of time on," New said.

* * *

This special report from Capitol Publications' Education Research Group is intended to help you meet the challenges of the new law.

It describes innovative programs you can duplicate in whole or in part. It probes the effects of the new law on staffing, enrollment and funding. And it keys in on how states that already have programs are managing them.

Chapter One gives you an overview of the legislative history of P.L. 99-457 and the funding issues that surround it.

Chapter Two takes you into the newest program, that for children from birth through age 2. It examines who these children are, presents convincing research showing that early intervention works, and gives tips on starting infant and toddler programs from states that already are serving the youngest children.

Chapter Three explores the challenges of serving handicapped preschoolers, particularly in defining least restrictive environment when your state has no mandated programs for nonhandicapped preschoolers.

Chapter Four makes recommendations for coping with the dramatic shortage of qualified personnel in infant intervention, preschool, related services and medical settings.

Chapter Five ties in the critical issue of child care, and Chapter Six discusses parents' strong role in setting up programs for their children. Both chapters point out the need to get the entire family involved in the education and care of the youngest handicapped children.

Chapters Two through Six conclude with "From Our Rolodex," a listing of people who have agreed to be contacts for you, and one or more case studies of successful programs.

The appendices provide you with the complete text of the law, as well as charts, tables and resource listings.

* * *

Many people assisted us in the research and writing of this book. Too many to name here (though they are named throughout the book) are the dozens of people who spent hours with us on the telephone or in person, explaining their programs or discussing the challenges they see ahead in implementing the new law. We would, however, like to single out for thanks several people who helped us steer our research in the right direction: Sharon Walsh of NASDSE, Gloria Harbin and Pat Trohanis of START, early childhood consultant Barbara J. Smith, Peggy Stephens of Kentucky and John Clark of Nebraska.

Helping us with the writing were James Buie and Carol Ellison. Jim, a staff writer with the Education Research Group and editor of *How To Evaluate Education Programs,* researched and wrote Case Study 3.3. Carol, a former education reporter with the *Cincinnati Post* who is now based in New Jersey, researched and wrote Case Studies 3.2 and 6.1.

Much credit goes to Education Research Group managing editor Leslie A. Ratzlaff, who edited the manuscript and coordinated the production of the report. Thanks also to editorial assistant Christopher Grasso; production manager Rosette Graham; typesetter Cynthia Peters; graphic artist Linda C. McDonald; and our marketing and circulation staff: Kristan S. Winters, Tammy Vagias, Ellen Carroll, Allison Sator, Barbara L. Davis, Gloria Smith, Joan Rodriguez and Robin Carey. We'd like to acknowledge the assistance and cooperation of the *Report on Preschool Programs* managing staff, Mary Klein and Charles Dervarics. Finally, to our publisher, Helen Hoart, thanks for giving us the encouragement and support we needed to undertake this project.

Roberta Weiner and Jane Koppelman

Chapter One

Overview

Probe an early intervention advocate and you'll get this visceral response: legislation to serve the youngest handicapped children was long overdue.

Probe an educator with responsibility for children of all ages and abilities and you'll get this one: we can't afford it.

No one will admit to opposing the concept behind the 1986 Education of the Handicapped Act (EHA) Amendments, P.L. 99-457, which provide strong financial incentives for states to extend special education and related services down to age 3 and establish a new grant program to help states serve handicapped infants and toddlers.

But questions and concerns about implementing the legislation are rampant, much as they were with the passage in 1975 of the Education for All Handicapped Children Act, P.L. 94-142, also an amendment to EHA. At the top of both lists is how society will pay for the programs.

As with P.L. 94-142, the noise will die down and the slow, steady process of implementing a new program will begin. But, also as with P.L. 94-142, it's likely the funding questions will never end.

Why Now?

The concept of providing early intervention services to handicapped children has been before Congress, in one form or another, for two decades. In 1975, an early form of the bill that was to become P.L. 94-142 included a requirement to serve children starting at age 3. But, in a compromise that may have assured the bill's passage, Congress deleted it, and the final law gave states discretion over serving preschoolers.

"The period of time that we're in is one of coalescing, bringing together the best of what we know in terms of working with very young children and their families," said Pascal Trohanis, director of the State Technical Assistance Resource Team (START) at the Frank Porter Graham Child Development Center at the University of North Carolina in Chapel Hill. START helps states implement programs for young handicapped children through a cooperative agreement with the U.S. Education Department.

Fifteen years of demonstration projects and other research coupled with a growing political interest in the needs of children and families, particularly the growth in awareness of the need for child care, "all came together to improve and consolidate what we know to create new and better services for children and families," Trohanis said.

In addition, said Frederick Weintraub, assistant exective director of the Council for Exceptional Children (CEC), "there has been a growing acceptance" outside the special education community of early intervention. For instance, he noted, the 1986 National Governors' Association report, "Time For Results: The Governors' 1991 Report on Education," called on states to develop new initiatives to help at-risk preschool children prepare for school.

Another crucial factor, said Weintraub, was the commitment from two key congressmen: Sen. Lowell Weicker, R-Conn., and Rep. Pat Williams, D-Mont., both strong advocates for handicapped children.

Up to now, neither lawmaker "had anything that they could say was their big contribution," said Weintraub. Before passage of P.L. 99-457, "all they could say was, 'I had good stewardship of the committee and preserved the work of 1975.' They both wanted to leave a mark."

Weintraub credited Williams' "willingness to play teamwork," along with "the combination of Lowell Weicker personality and Lowell Weicker powerful," which, he said, means "basically Lowell Weicker gets what Lowell Weicker wants. When you consider you pass this thing through the Senate with 30 seconds of debate or whatever and it's unanimous, that's a testament to Lowell Weicker." In fact, both chambers passed the measure with no amendments and little debate.

Weicker has been the most influential lawmaker in special education since the early 1980s, as chair of the Senate Subcommittee on the Handicapped and, since 1983, also chairman of the education appropriations subcommittee. Some speculate that Weicker decided to make preschool his number one issue for 1986 because he suspected the Senate might turn Democrat when the 100th Congress convened in 1987, as it did, and with the transfer would go his committee chairmanships.

Also critical to the bill's passage at this time was the growing movement in states toward enacting early childhood programs, said Barbara J. Smith, an early childhood consultant who is a member of the national executive board of CEC's Division for Early Childhood.

John Clark, 1986-87 president of the National Association of State Directors of Special Education, agreed. Particularly in the preschool area, "It's in the same spirit as [P.L.] 94-142," said the assistant director of special education in Nebraska. The concept, he said, was, "Let's finish the task that was embarked on by states already."

Congress based its approval of the legislation, in part, on U.S. Education Department data that showed states were serving more than 75 percent, or 260,000, of the estimated 330,000 handicapped children ages 3 through 5 in the nation.

When it appeared the legislation had a chance of becoming law, the final step, Smith said, was a major grassroots effort by parents and professionals. "The people in the communities started calling their congressmen, saying, 'We're here as resources.' When congressmen went home for the 1986 Labor Day holiday, a lot of them were visited by parents and advocates at the local level and were taken for visits at the programs."

Soon after its return from the September recess, Congress approved P.L. 99-457 (then S. 2294), Smith noted. The House passed the compromise measure Sept. 23, 1986; the Senate, which had passed the original bill in June 1986, approved the compromise one day after the House. President Reagan signed the bill into law Oct. 8, 1986, after heavy telephone lobbying by that same grassroots network.

P.L. 99-457 reauthorizes the discretionary programs of the Education of the Handicapped Act for five years and sets up two major new programs:

1. A new state grant program for handicapped infants and toddlers from birth through age 2. States that want to participate must designate a lead agency, develop a statewide plan and agreements for interagency participation, require individualized family service plans for each child and his or her family, and guarantee full services within four years. P.L. 99-457 requires that services be provided to families at no cost except where federal or state law provides for a system of payments by families, including a schedule of sliding fees.

2. Strong incentives for states to serve handicapped children ages 3 through 5 by school year 1990-91. From fiscal year 1990 on, grants may be made only to states that assure the availability of a free appropriate public education for all handicapped children ages 3 through 5. The requirement will be delayed one year if Congress doesn't appropriate at least $656 million for fiscal years 1987, 1988 and 1989 combined, and $306 million for fiscal 1990. It increases funding for preschool children already served from about $100 per child to $300 per child in fiscal 1987, $400 per child in 1988 and $500 per child in 1989, topping off at $1,000 in 1990. It also sets up a new funding mechanism — $3,800 per new child — for helping states serve children who are currently not receiving any services.

In the final analysis, Smith and Weintraub both credited the victory to good timing. "I'm always a believer that things happen because of time and circumstances," said Weintraub. "The political leadership was right and the constituency communities that fought so hard and long on the early childhood issue were willing to accept something that was not all of what they wanted, but was good."

Costs

In characteristically direct remarks after the bill was cleared for President Reagan's signature, Sen. Weicker said, "Make no mistake that today we send a message to the handicapped citizens of our nation that their needs are not going to be sacrificed at the altar of budget cuts or educational reforms."

Some school administrators turn Weicker's remarks on their head, saying they're afraid education reforms and services to nonhandicapped children are going to be sacrificed to the needs of handicapped children.

The debate over funding for special education—thanks to Weicker, virtually the only education program to escape federal budget cuts in the Reagan years—is a neverending one. General educators consistently harken back to Congress's broken promise to pick up 40 percent of the average per pupil costs of P.L. 94-142. Special educators and child development specialists, equally disappointed at Congress's unfulfilled promise (the federal government's share has gone no higher than 12 percent), say it's unethical to let funding difficulties stand in the way of programs that can change the course of a handicapped child's life.

Don Sheldon, deputy executive director of the American Association of School Administrators, while quick to support the concept of early intervention, has a very real fear that schools will be forced into "siphoning off funds from general education to provide for this new mandate."

He does not believe school districts will opt out of the program, saying they will "comply, as they always have with mandates. Quite candidly, there's no choice."

Instead, "given the limited resources of most school districts, without an additional referendum of some kind, they're going to have to utilize existing funds, and that means drawing down funds from other program areas."

Some districts, he said, may eliminate certain extracurricular activities; others may eliminate some elective programs; others may have no problem at all. "I don't know the effect on specific school districts, but having been there as a school superintendent, I understand the kind of tradeoffs that can occur when there is a new mandate. The impact on programs can be very dramatic or can be minimal, depending on the resources of specific school districts."

Michael Casserly, senior associate for legislation and research of the Council of the Great City Schools, agreed with Sheldon that funding will be the major impediment to implementing P.L. 99-457. "We hope Congress is good on their promise for more money in this area. If history is any indication, they're probably good for some of it."

Despite funding difficulties, Casserly said, "I suspect that most cities will not opt out because most of them have some experience in programming at that level and their capacities are greater" than smaller districts. On the other hand, "It's a substantial new set of requirements at a time that city school systems continue to be under financial stress."

James Oglesby, secretary/treasurer of the National School Boards Association (NSBA) and a school board member from Columbia, Mo., said, "I feel pretty much as I did about [P.L.] 94-142. 94-142 was never fully funded. The last thing we wanted to see was another bill floating through without being fully funded."

Oglesby pointed out that schools are not set up to handle infants and toddlers. In an appendix to Oglesby's congressional testimony on P.L. 99-457, NSBA said it believes Congress underestimated the start-up costs to schools in such areas as construction, transportation, equipment and staffing. Even school districts that now provide services don't necessarily use all the federally mandated procedures, serve all categories of students, or serve all students within categories, noted NSBA.

States currently suffering from a depressed property tax base, such as Oklahoma, Wyoming and the Dakotas, Oglesby said, are having trouble paying their bills as it is. "So to lay on additional requirements at a time when they're trying to handle their regular budgetary programs doesn't make a whole lot of sense."

Oglesby sees the new law as one more example of the federal government telling states what their priorities should be in education. Federal priorities, he said, "may or may not be of the most high priority within the local community." He sees a conflict with education reform movements currently going on in many states. "As we attempt reform, restructuring programs for college bound students, consider extending the school day or year, you're talking about major resources, while you're asking us to bring on a new program."

Oglesby, who has been a school board member since 1974, just laughed when asked whether schools could opt out of the program.

He repeatedly said, "It's a federal law, isn't it?"

"The only thing we have to base it on is past precedent, [P.L.] 94-142. In some form or other, they ended up participating in 94-142. It's a federal law. Do you comply or not? The option that they [schools] have is if you do not comply in this program, they [the federal government] can withdraw your other federal funds" for preschool programs.

Local special educators also view the funding with some alarm. Jim L. Newby, director of special services for the Oklahoma City Public Schools, said, "If in fact appropriations are made at levels proposed by [P.L.] 99-457, it would certainly go a long way toward offsetting costs. However, I think many LEAs [local education agencies] across the country are waiting to see that happen, if it happens."

Of course, even with full appropriations, "there is no way" it will cover the funding needed and thus, state and local dollars are needed, Newby noted. In Oklahoma, he said, that's unlikely. "States in the Oil Belt are hard pressed at this time. Competition for funding at the state level will become more intense." Oklahoma currently mandates services from age 4, except for children who are both deaf and blind or who "fail to thrive."

Oglesby brought up another issue in his testimony on the bill before the House Select Education Subcommittee, where he urged members to consider the issue of insurance as part of the funding picture. "There's no question about it, it's been ignored," he said. "Districts are having problems with insurance, the insurance industry is topsy turvy. Liability depends on risk and we're dealing with high-risk students." Oglesby believes a small number of high-risk students will skew schools' total insurance programs to the extent that some districts that are currently self-insured will not be able to manage their program with the new requirement.

Oglesby notes that some districts in midwestern states have just 50 or 60 children, with a total budget of no more than $120,000. A program for infants and toddlers "could cost them more than their existing budget," he said. "They just don't have the resources, nor do they have the mechanism to raise the resources. In some cases, they have difficulties providing" a kindergarten through grade 12 program.

Weintraub views the situation differently. "You have this imagery that there is this single pot of money that handicapped kids sneak into school in the middle of the night and steal. I didn't hear anybody say they built a new science lab in the high school and that took away from handicapped kids; they gave money to the football team and that took away from handicapped kids.

"It's as if somehow the money all belongs to them and handicapped kids take it away from them; that handicapped kids can have their needs served only if they get their own money. I don't hear them saying if you want to set up a Latin class you kids get your own money. Yet this game goes on all the time."

Barbara Smith thinks the best strategy for getting more money is for schools to wholeheartedly throw themselves into the program.

She explains: "The more states and more communities that attempt to meet the early intervention needs of this nation, the more federal resources will be available. My concern at this point when I hear some people say that they're concerned about even participating in the program because of unstable funding, my response is if you don't participate, that really jeopardizes the funding. The fewer states that participate, the fewer advocates we have talking to the Congress, the fewer arguments we have from year to year."

If states get in there now and participate, Smith said, "we can start to build a database, build numbers of kids. We don't know how many kids we're talking about, particularly in the infant area. So the more states that get in there now and start counting the kids, start finding the kids, in a year or two down the road we'll have hard and fast numbers" to take back to Congress. "To not participate now is really shooting ourselves in the foot."

But more than just a funding issue, Smith sees an ethical issue.

"To me, now that we know how important early intervention is, for any professional to say we should withhold programs for lack of federal funds, is not professional," Smith said.

"We have to ask people to look at their professional and program priorities as well as their personal priorities. When they go to the election booth as an individual citizen, are they thinking about funding for early intervention? When they are working on campaigns or when they have the opportunity to influence elected officials, are they thinking about early intervention resources? Educators are citizens and they vote," she said. "I think the resources are possible, but I think it requires that we really look at our program priorities and our own personal political behavior. And if somebody is saying they do think early intervention is important, then I say, 'Does your behavior show that?'"

Smith's view is shared by the researcher considered to be the leader in the early intervention field, Dr. T. Berry Brazelton. "Reducing the anguish and the opportunity to salvage children at risk is what we ought to be after," said Brazelton, chief of the child development unit at the Boston Children's Hospital. "Let's increase our resources, reorganize our thinking. [The money we spend on] one bomb or one missile would take care of this whole program."

Brazelton, also a professor of pediatrics at Harvard Medical School, points out that spending the money in the earliest years of life is "obviously a way for the federal government, for all of us, to save an enormous amount of money" later in the person's life. For example, it costs an average of $106 a day to pay for the institutionalization of a mentally retarded person, according to Kris Rogge, a developmental disabilities program specialist in the Department of Health and Human Services' Office of Human Development.

Phase-In Time

Because of all the issues that have been raised, many school officials believe the phase-in time allowed in the law is too short. "There's no way it can be sufficient," said Oglesby, considering the myriad concerns he has raised, including staffing, insurance, facilities and curricula.

Lawrence Gloeckler, state director of special education in New York, is one of many state special education directors also very concerned about getting geared up fast enough to start using money in September 1987 while final regulations won't be available until just two months earlier. "It's going to be a difficult decision for states," particularly those who need to adopt legislation while their legislature may not be in session, he said.

"A Small Miracle"

Despite the challenges schools and other providers face in meeting the requirements of P.L. 99-457, a great deal of satisfaction exists in knowing that public policy has moved in the direction of helping the youngest handicapped children.

Putting it simply and directly was Dr. Allen Crocker, director of the developmental evaluation clinic at Boston Children's Hospital: "It really thrills one," he said. "It's a small miracle."

Chapter Two

Birth Through Two: Serving Handicapped Infants And Toddlers

At Howard University Hospital in Washington, D.C., the premature babies are eerily silent, the piercing sounds of their monitors and the nurses' radios taking the place of the healthy crying of the full-term infants in the nearby nursery.

The scenario, repeated daily in the 594 infant intensive care units across the country, represents one extreme of serving handicapped infants and toddlers. But the medical model for helping handicapped children too sick to leave the hospital is just one aspect of serving this population. Programs for infants and toddlers may take place in a child's home or in a school, child care center or other facility. Services may range in intensity from round-the-clock medical care to once-a-week sessions with a physical therapist.

The 1986 amendments to the Education of the Handicapped Act establish a new state grant program for handicapped infants and toddlers. Its aim: to help states provide early intervention services to children who are developmentally delayed or who have conditions that suggest a "high probability" of resulting in a delay. States also have the option of serving children who are at risk of "substantial" developmental delays if early intervention is not provided (the complete text of the law is in Appendix A).

In recent years, research has shown that early intervention dramatically improves children's physical, cognitive and social abilities, minimizing the effects of existing and potential handicaps. "We're learning scientifically that starting early makes a significant difference in outcome," said Dr. T. Berry Brazelton, a leading early intervention researcher who is chief of the child development unit at Boston Children's Hospital.

Brazelton, who also is a professor of pediatrics at Harvard Medical School, noted another reason the issue has come to the fore is because medical science is able to save increasing numbers of low birthweight and other at-risk babies. To illustrate, in 1960, 28 percent of low-birthweight babies were still alive at age one, according to the National Center for Health Statistics. In 1980, the center said, more than 50 percent of these babies celebrated a first birthday.

And the numbers of babies that live continue to go up, according to Brazelton. "We're saving smaller and smaller babies. The kind of brains we're leaving them with are better and better. This makes it really worthwhile to get in and do something for them. We have babies with good brains but they may have social difficulties."

Basically, said Brazelton, early intervention can do two things: prevent many physical and psychological disorders, and mitigate their effects on the quality of life of the person involved.

For example, scientists have learned how to repair or make up for an impaired central nervous system, which — if the intervention starts early — can actually arrest some learning disabilities, Brazelton said. And babies given the proper stimulation from birth can develop stronger self images that can help them work through the limitations of a handicap as they get older, he said.

With a handicap such as blindness, children can learn to compensate by being trained to use with increased sensitivity their hearing, sense of touch and the vibrations of their own voice, Brazelton explained in "Early Intervention: What Does It Mean?" An instance of this is "radar vision" in one 14-month-old blind infant, "who vocalized as she walked and never ran into tables, rounded corners of doors by the differences in reverberations as her vocalizations bounced off nearby objects," he wrote in the article, published in *Theory and Research in Behavioral Pediatrics.*

With such remarkable capability to improve children's potential, "it becomes more and more important that we be able to evaluate at-risk infants as early as possible with an eye to more sophisticated preventive and therapeutic approaches, before failure systems and the expectation to fail become established," wrote Brazelton.

The House Education and Labor Committee agreed. In its report accompanying the bill that was to become P.L. 99-457, the committee said that, based on the research, "an overwhelming case exists for expanding and improving the provision of early intervention and preschool programs." The committee quoted the U.S. Education Department's seventh annual report to Congress: "The studies have shown that the earlier intervention is started, the greater is the ultimate dollar savings and the higher is the rate of educational attainment."

Selecting The Best Programs

In fact, researchers have moved way beyond the question of whether early intervention helps handicapped children. They are now grappling with the question of what kinds of programs best help handicapped children.

"Posing the overall question is a little bit foolish," said Phillip S. Strain, director of the Early Childhood Research Institute at the University of Pittsburgh. "You have to say, if you design a maximally

Birth Through Two

effective program, one that's state of the art, what can you expect from that?"

The question then becomes, how do educators and others interested in setting up programs for infants and toddlers find a state-of-the-art program?

"To get that information, you have to look around and you have to do some detective work because not all of the outcomes you'd be interested in are available in any one particular study," said Strain. "But when you do that detective work, you see effects range very widely for kids. There are significant changes in children's cognitive skills, their social skills, their motor functioning."

Other studies show "significant changes" in terms of lessening stress on the child's parents, Strain said. And still others show a "reasonable portion" of seriously handicapped youngsters being educated in a regular class setting, he said.

But more research is needed. Researchers say an added benefit of the law will be that, by increasing the numbers of children served, it will provide a better research base for making future decisions about the kinds of programs that work best.

"There is not a lot of scientific data about which services are most cost-effective. Whether it's the most intensive, whether it's home-based versus center-based, whether it's one day a week versus five days a week," said Karl R. White, director of the Early Intervention Effectiveness Institute at Utah State University. "I hope the law will be implemented in a way that we can systematically collect that kind of data so we can know more about what will help kids the most."

Instead, the key argument currently for early intervention for handicapped children "is similar to the logic in treating cancer patients. Twenty years ago, we knew people with cancer were going to die. So we began looking for ways to alleviate the suffering, reduce the incidence and hopefully cure cancer," he said.

"We didn't do that by saying let's put no money in cancer treatment programs. We didn't say let's randomly select people to be treated or not treated. We did say let's try this treatment, that treatment, we systematically looked at alternative treatments," White said. "And the same is true for early intervention. Handicapped children clearly have some problems and their families have some problems in managing their problems. The issue shouldn't be, 'Do we help or don't we?' It should be 'What type of help would be most cost-beneficial in the long-term?' Given the fact of limited resources, we want to focus on those types of intervention that are most cost-effective."

Without the needed research already in place, educators and others who want to set up infant and toddler programs are "going to have to base it all on professional judgments," White said. "And there's nothing wrong with that as long as you implement it in such a way that you can collect data on what works best with whom. There are a lot of models out there. People have been doing early intervention for a good 10 years now. There's not a scarcity of programs, there's a scarcity of good data."

Whom To Serve?

Developmental Delay Some infants and toddlers are relatively easy to diagnose. They're blind or deaf or have an obvious physical impairment. Others may be delayed somewhat in their development, but that may be just about all the physician or child development specialists can say.

Because it is difficult to properly diagnose or label a handicapped infant or toddler as having a particular handicap, and because such diagnoses or labels can be impossible to discard even if proven incorrect or unnecessary later in the child's life, P.L. 99-457 adds the term "developmental delay" as a way to serve children from birth through age 2 without labeling them. Each state, as part of its comprehensive system for serving infants and toddlers with disabilities, is to come up with its own definition of the term developmental delay.

Some educators fear the use of the term will open the floodgates, letting in children who may simply be slow learners and have no place in programs for handicapped children.

But early childhood specialists believe the use of the term is important for young children, and advocate that its use be extended through age 5. In fact, experts have debated for more than 20 years the merits of labeling any children, saying it can lead adults to lower their expectations for the children and for the children themselves to lower their self image. For young children, the concern over mislabeling just adds to the arguments against labeling.

"Children under age 6 develop very unevenly," said Barbara J. Smith, a consultant in early childhood policy who is on the national executive board of the Council for Exceptional Children's (CEC) Division for Early Childhood. "Their development fluctuates rapidly. They can show a lot of the same kinds of symptoms for various reasons. They can be showing delays in development either because they are mentally retarded, have cerebral palsy or are learning disabled, none of which is clear because they are so young and responses are not so developed."

Smith is among those who believe "it's difficult to label 6- or 10-year-olds, but impossible to label some 3-year-olds," calling such attempts nothing more than "a shot in the dark."

Not only that, Smith said, but, bearing in mind that the label may be inaccurate or inapplicable down the road, "if you place a label on a child such as learning disabled, mentally retarded, it's sometimes difficult to get rid of the label. In fact, the child's delay may have been totally remediated but you can't get rid of the label."

While the law did not insert the term developmental delay in the 3 through 5 program, it did amend P.L. 94-142 to say 3- through 5-year-olds do not have to be labeled to be served. P.L. 94-142 requires states to count their children by category to be funded. Under the 1986 amendments, they just need to turn in the total number of children for 3- through 5-year-olds, while still dividing the children age 6 and older into categories.

Smith, who along with CEC had argued for placing the term developmental delay in P.L. 99-457 for 3- through 5-year-olds, argues that states who already have gone from a categorical to developmentally delayed criterion saw only a slight increase in the numbers of children who qualified. "In some states, it didn't go up at all," said Smith. "The whole issue of will it open up floodgates is a false one. It didn't happen."

In fact, when states used the noncategorical approach, they had to develop eligibility criteria for the definition of developmentally delayed, which turned out to be more stringent than the categorical approach, she said. For instance, Smith said, a typical state policy for developmentally delayed says the child must be evaluated by a multidisciplinary team, a variety of assessment instruments must be used, the delay must be one or two standard deviations below normal on one or more instruments and, sometimes, in more than one area.

At Risk Some of the premature infants in the Howard University intensive care unit will grow up to be just fine. Many others will have a disability of some sort. But that's just it. You can't say that just because a baby is premature its development will necessarily be delayed, even if its birthweight is what's statistically considered "low"—less than three pounds, four ounces.

What you can say is that the child will be at risk of a developmental delay.

Under P.L. 99-457, states are to serve children who "have a diagnosed physical or mental condition which has a high probability of resulting in developmental delay." States are allowed—but not required—to serve children "at risk of having substantial developmental delays if early intervention services are not provided."

Who are those children? Child development specialists typically divide handicapped and at-risk children into three categories:

1. The first, and smallest group, includes children who are born

with obvious disabilities. This includes children born deaf, blind, severely physically disabled or mentally retarded.

2. The second, larger, group includes children who are biologically at risk. They are born with conditions that foreshadow the probability of problems occuring. They include the low-birthweight babies and children born with fetal alcohol syndrome or other drug-related problems.

3. The third, and by far the largest, group includes children considered to be environmentally at risk. These are children born into living conditions that would suggest that unless someone intervenes with them and their families, they will have problems. The group expands with varying definitions. It can include children born to an adolescent mother or into poverty. Estimates of the size of this group range from 3 percent to 10 percent of the population. States have the option of serving children in this category.

For example, in a family where the parents are not employed "there is a greater potential of abuse," said Frederick Weintraub, CEC's assistant executive director. "We know that in families without good nutrition and good medical care, children develop poorly." Exacerbating the problem, Weintraub said, is that adults in those environments tend to have more children than adults in other environments.

Those who evaluate children suspected of having developmental delays look at all three categories, explained Dr. Allen Crocker, director of the developmental evaluation clinic at Boston Children's Hospital. Crocker, whose clinic evaluates children who have or are suspected to have a developmental delay, said he can predict an "increased likelihood" of a delay "when the number of abnormal variables in the infant's background exceeds that of the average population."

Sometimes a child may fall into more than one category, said Crocker, such as if the mother is an alcoholic so the baby has fetal alcohol syndrome (biological risk) and the mother has problems parenting (environmental risk).

The chances for success of a baby who is biologically at risk are much greater, Crocker noted, "when the baby goes home to a well-structured household with all the appropriate amenities and support, than if you send the child home to a single-room, cold-water walkup with an unmarried mother. So you have a tendency in child development to have a compounding of problems. If a baby is at risk in more than one category, you could very well claim that the baby is in double jeopardy."

Another consideration is that children in category one — those with obvious disabilities — are not necessarily the most in need;

conversely, children in category three—those environmentally at risk—are not always the least in need, said Dr. Jack P. Shonkoff, an associate professor of pediatrics and principal investigator/project director of the Early Intervention Collaborative Study at the University of Massachusetts Medical School.

"If we were to look at this question from a public policy point of view and decide that we really want to target our resources on that part of the population that is most likely to have the greatest problems later, it's very possible that some children considered at risk represent a more vulnerable group than some children with identified disabilities," said Shonkoff. "Certainly children with specifically diagnosed disabilities need early intervention services and will continue to need help later on. However, it doesn't necessarily follow that the most vulnerable population are children with identified disabilities. In fact, establishing a cutoff based solely on diagnosis means that we may actually exclude some who are more likely to have problems."

Shonkoff added, "As much as people would like it to be that simple—to make decisions based strictly on a diagnosis—it doesn't work that way in the real world."

Nor is he recommending to turn the formula on its head and serve at-risk children first. Rather, each category includes some children who have lesser needs and others who have more serious needs, Shonkoff said.

"P.L. 99-457 focuses on children with identified disabilities and children at risk for substantial special needs later. But children without diagnosed disabilities are difficult to define in a regulation," he said.

While acknowledging that it would be "politically impossible" to mandate comprehensive services for all young children at risk for problems, "in the best of all possible worlds, I would support a range of intervention alternatives whenever vulnerability has been identified," Shonkoff said. The key, he added, "is careful and sensitive consideration of the goals of the service system. If the goals are to serve those with the greatest needs, or those who can benefit the most, we must go beyond specific diagnosis as the single criterion for service delivery."

States were given the discretion to serve environmentally at-risk children for two reasons, said Weintraub. First, some states—Maine, he said, is one example—"have decided to be rather creative and to try to put together early intervention models that are not solely" for children with acknowledged handicaps, and Congress did not want to penalize them by excluding at-risk children. Second, it would have been too difficult politically to extend a mandate to the larger population, so what's left is a compromise that says environmentally at-risk children are included at state discretion, he said.

In Maine, the focus has been on the preschool years, but the state is moving toward serving the youngest children. And the state has a "significant interest and focus on the at-risk population, which we define very broadly," said David Stockford, state director of special education in Maine. The state is trying to look at the whole family situation, "including looking at the relationship between the infant and family members," he said.

Part of Maine's support for serving at-risk children, Stockford said, stems from its work with school-age children, many of whom might not have needed special education had they been served from an early age.

In addition, he said, Maine's Department of Human Services has been focusing on the issue of child abuse and neglect. "What you see are young people who exhibit significant problems that do interfere with their learning," he said. Instead of ignoring those problems and letting many of these children end up in institutions, the state has begun to "look very carefully" at expanding its programs for at-risk children.

It's unclear at this point how many states will follow Maine's example and how many will stick with a more conservative definition of eligibility. "States that are more economically sound at this point or in the next five years, or are poised for economic growth, might be better able to address the broader needs of children who are at risk than are other states that, because of economic circumstances, may prohibit some of that faster growth or faster development," noted Pascal Trohanis, director of the State Technical Assistance Resource Team (START) at the Frank Porter Graham Child Development Center at the University of North Carolina in Chapel Hill.

Existing Programs

Services for handicapped infants from birth are mandated in seven states—Iowa, Maryland, Michigan, Nebraska, New Jersey, Oregon and South Dakota—and three territories—American Samoa, the U.S. Trust Territories and Guam—according to the U.S. Education Department (see Appendix B). Virginia mandates services from age 2. But the vast majority of states start their mandates at ages 3, 4, 5 or 6.

That wide variety in service delivery was the primary reason P.L. 99-457's new program for infants and toddlers was needed, said the

University of Pittsburgh's Phillip Strain. "Right now there's a pretty significant disparity over who gets services and who doesn't as a function of which state you live in, which is not a particularly equitable arrangement," he said. The new law "really opens some doors for the first time."

P.L. 99-457 adds a new Part H to the Education of the Handicapped Act that establishes a multidisciplinary, interagency program of discretionary grants to states for serving children from birth through age 2. To be eligible for the grants (estimated grants to each state for fiscal 1987 appear in Appendix C), each state's program for infants and toddlers must include the following 14 minimum components within four years:

1. A definition of developmentally delayed.
2. A timetable for services to all in need in the state.
3. Requirements for comprehensive, multidisciplinary evaluations of each handicapped infant or toddler and the needs of families.
4. Requirements for a written, individualized family service plan (IFSP) for each handicapped infant or toddler, to be evaluated yearly.
5. A comprehensive child find and referral system.
6. A public awareness program.
7. A central directory of services, resources, experts and research.
8. A comprehensive system of personnel development.
9. A single line of responsibility in a lead agency chosen by the governor.
10. A policy on contracting with local service providers.
11. A procedure for timely reimbursement of funds.
12. Procedural safeguards.
13. Policies and procedures for personnel standards.
14. A data collection system.

States can measure themselves against these 14 points to see how much farther they need to go to take part in the program for infants and toddlers, said Trohanis.

"States certainly can add to those components," he said, noting that some states are looking at transportation as a fifteenth component. In addition, the law makes it clear that states must make available a continuum of early intervention services, although that may not be obvious from the 14 components, Trohanis said.

* * *

Even states with long-established programs beginning at birth have much to do before their programs include everything the law's 14 components require.

Nebraska In Nebraska, which has mandated services from birth since the late 1970s, the state uses handicapping labels on all students from birth and thus must grapple with defining developmental delay. "I look for a very vigorous professional debate," said John Clark, assistant director of his state education department's Special Education Branch.

Opposition exists to changing the current use of labels, particularly from the state legislature, which "wants to be sure that only kids who are truly handicapped receive the benefits of the dollars available," Clark said. Practitioners, on the other hand, would like to go to a noncategorical approach because they share the experts' concerns about mislabeling young children.

Nebraska also must work on the individualized family service plan (IFSP) concept, including case management for each family. "Our focus is on an IEP [the individualized education plan required under P.L. 94-142]. IFSP broadens that," Clark noted. "I've heard a number of concerns over just what case management means. Who will be responsible? Are we going to allow people to be very intrusive?"

Overall, Clark doesn't think his state will have to "undo anything that affects students." But state administration will have to change, he said. "We'll have to do more recordkeeping, more interaction with other agencies. We'll have to create an advisory group to oversee all of this."

Delaware In Delaware, the overall mandate for serving handicapped children starts at age 4. But the state mandates services from birth for deaf, blind, deaf-blind and autistic children and from age 3 for orthopedically impaired, severely handicapped and trainable mentally handicapped children.

Deborah Ziegler, director of the Delaware early childhood state plan grant and preschool incentive grant, said the state is moving quickly to adapt its system to the new law.

"We are looking to change all our classification systems to go along with developmentally delayed. We have state legislation in to mandate services in our state down to birth, for all handicapped and developmentally delayed children across any category," she said.

Delaware's lead agency is the Department of Public Instruction, of which Ziegler is a part. "Definitely, we wanted it. Other agencies were interested in it as well. We're certainly very excited" about taking on the birth through 2 program, Ziegler said.

Her state in 1985 started an experimental program for infants and toddlers in Kent and Sussex counties. The program, which is run cooperatively by the Department of Public Instruction and the Department of Public Health, is called Specialized Tots Assessment and Readiness Training. In addition, the Department of Public Instruction initiated a birth through 2 program in December 1986 in Delaware's third county, Newcastle.

The state also has a central tracking system for all handicapped, developmentally delayed or at-risk children from birth through age 6. All agencies, both public and private, participate, Ziegler said. The system, which is on a central mainframe computer with wide access, includes a service record and a client record, with the parent's name and address, the child's handicapping condition, the service provided and by what agency.

The system's purpose is to "plan for future services, to cut down on duplication of services as well as not to lose track of the child," said Ziegler. Because of laws guaranteeing confidentiality to handicapped children, an agency must have parental permission to include a child on the computer.

Her "biggest task is to come up with an interagency model. We have some initiatives now, but as in many other states, we need to put it together much better than now."

"It's very difficult to predict how long it will take" to come into compliance with the new law, Ziegler said. "Some things are in place because we are serving some kids under 5." A rough estimate, she said, would be that it will take "a good three years to put into place. You just don't know."

Iowa Delaware's estimate of three years to put its program in place is Joan Turner Clary's estimate of the shortest amount of time it could take to put together a program from scratch. Clary, early childhood special education program consultant in Iowa's Department of Education, said Iowa's mandate to serve handicapped children from birth passed in 1974. They began to put it into place in 1975 and finished in 1980.

"I felt we had sufficient time," Clary said. "I would say you couldn't do it in less than three years. It would depend on the state support you had. We had all the support in the world and also the funding."

As in Nebraska, Clary sees formal case management and implementation of the IFSP as Iowa's biggest challenge.

"We see that as being extremely difficult," she said. "For example, there are issues of who's going to make the determination of what is needed. We really have very grave concerns about whether we would want to try to get other agencies to provide services. Who would make the final decision? Who would be sued? If agencies are working under an interagency system and there's conflict among representatives on the council, would education or other agencies be obliged to discontinue services based upon the council's decision, even though it might be contrary to the current delivery system?"

Clary said she thinks "a lot of states that are just now getting into this don't even realize the questions that are there, looming. We have been in a position for many years to be sued by parents. So we have all the due process procedures in place. I think a lot of states maybe do not totally realize the implications or the ramifications of all of this."

States Without Mandates States that have no program in place have very little to say about the birth through 2 program. An informal survey of state special education directors at a November 1986 conference of the National Association of State Directors of Special Education (NASDSE) elicited the following two genres of replies: "Who knows?" and "Thank God we've got four years."

As of February 1987, 25 states had told the U.S. Education Department they planned to participate in the program. None had yet declined to participate.

In Illinois, the state special education department wants a mandated program from birth — the mandate is now from age 3 — and is working on a study, due in January 1989, to gather data to defend its position, said Jonah Deppe, coordinator of the state's early intervention plan. "We believe the new law will be ammunition to help us get a mandate," probably by 1990-91, she said.

Trohanis believes leaving the birth through 2 system to each state has "pluses and minuses."

On the plus side, "Congress was very interested in allowing states to create systems that are responsive to their needs based on past history, based on their current array of services, resources and political context, so it will be truly unique to each jurisdiction," he said. On the negative side, "The reality in this country is people do move, so if people are to be defined in one jurisdiction one way, a neighboring state another way, it could be problematic for families."

Whose Job Is It?

While schools are in the spotlight because the infant and toddler program is part of a law — the Education of the Handicapped Act — that traditionally has focused on them, they are not necessarily intended to take care of the programs for the youngest children.

In fact, they may not even be the best ones to do it, said Dr. T. Berry Brazelton. "The only reason to use schools is that they're the institution that reaches everyone. They're set up. I'm not really sure they're the right ones" because they're "limited" to education, while programs for infants and toddlers must be multidisciplinary. Any agency, as long as it is multidisciplinary, can handle it, he said.

Many special educators — particularly those at the local level — say they don't want the responsibility. While the law does not require special education to take responsibility for infants and toddlers, many of those who work in schools anticipate much responsibility will come to them.

"I think it's a wonderful thing to identify at-risk children at an early age and give them services," said Hinda R. Miller, director of special education in the Upper Darby, Pa., School District, right outside Philadelphia. "But you don't need to automatically dump them into a special ed stream. Regular education needs to get more creative."

The law clearly calls for an interagency program of services that coordinates the payment from federal, state, local and private sources, including public and private insurance coverage. To be eligible for a grant, the state must establish an interagency coordinating council and give responsibility for the program to a lead agency, which can be the state education agency or any other appropriate agency.

Nonetheless, the National School Boards Association is also concerned that P.L. 99-457 could increase a school district's share of the cost to the extent that other agencies withdraw assistance, said James Oglesby, the organization's secretary/treasurer and a school board member from Missouri.

Sharing that concern is CEC. "Our experience with P.L. 94-142 has been that non-school-based resources that previously served handicapped children were redirected elsewhere when the responsibility for these children's education fell on the schools," Weintraub told Congress. "If this were to occur for infants the results would be disastrous. Neither states nor the federal government could afford to make up the difference."

The law does say — and the congressional report language backs it up strongly — that funds provided by P.L. 99-457 can't be substituted for existing public or private funds unless they are needed to prevent delay in services. The law also prohibits states from reducing Medicaid or Maternal and Child Health funds in response to the new funds.

The optimistic point of view comes from START's Trohanis. "I think special education is one of a number of partners in the establishment, maintenance and operation of a comprehensive service delivery system," he said. "I think states have an opportunity to determine" what each program can best contribute, including special education, social services, maternal and child health, EPSDT (the Early Periodic Screening, Diagnosis and Treatment program), developmental disabilities and mental health.

"I don't think the law says that special education has to do everything," said Trohanis. "I think there's a desire in this law to help look at the mosaic of all the different services that are available in a state and how agencies can work together."

Funding

Even before P.L. 99-457 became law, Congress had appropriated $50 million for the birth through 2 program for fiscal 1987. It authorized $75 million for fiscal 1988 and funds as needed thereafter. President Reagan has asked Congress to rescind the $50 million for fiscal 1987, but it is highly unlikely that the lawmakers will do so.

Congress did not expect the money to cover all services to children from birth through age 2. Instead, it's intended, as federal money typically is, to be seed money that encourages states to fund their own programs.

If states plan to spread the federal money across each child that needs services, "then the authorizations aren't high enough, the appropriations aren't high enough and they'll never be," said CEC's Weintraub. "If what states do is use that money for coordination, for plugging the gaps, for maximizing other resources, then it may make the difference to make it work." CEC, he said, "clearly viewed it as the latter."

"In the long run, $50 million may be too low, $100 million may be enough, I don't know what is the magic figure, it's not a billion. We'll have to look at it in the next couple of years," he said. Before the bill became law, the Congressional Budget Office estimated the birth through 2 program would cost $100 million.

A coalition of advocates is working on "a better way to finance" the birth through 2 program because traditional funding mechanisms will never provide enough money for the program, said Washington, D.C., attorney Martin Gerry. Gerry, who specializes in disability rights issues, said the youngest children "are not kids that require the average expenditure of [P.L.] 94-142 funds. You spend more on high-cost things like related services instead of relatively low-cost things like instruction." The real cost of doing the job, said Gerry, is "more than $100 million."

Transition And Interagency Coordination

Moving children smoothly from the birth through 2 programs into preschools or the public schools will be "a major challenge for states to wrestle with," said Trohanis. "I think there's a national awareness about this challenge of the transition issue. People are already thinking of creative and effective ways of ensuring that problems are minimized."

One solution Trohanis finds noteworthy is to create a state interagency council that cuts across infant, toddler and preschool concerns. While the infant and toddler program calls for a coordinating council, the preschool program doesn't because it assumes the youngsters will be covered by the education system and the umbrella of P.L. 94-142.

To lessen the transition problem, though, why not maintain that broader perspective and have a body that oversees both programs, Trohanis suggests.

North Carolina One state doing that is North Carolina, where the Department of Human Resources, in conjunction with the Department of Public Instruction, has proposed that their interagency coordinating council focus on handicapped children from birth through age 5.

"It's a way to give some continuity and coordination" to programs that will be run by two different departments," said Duncan Munn, chief of day services in the Division of Mental Health and Mental Retardation, a part of the human resources department. The governor has designated the Department of Human Resources as North Carolina's birth through 2 lead agency, while the Department of Public Instruction runs some programs for 3-, 4- and 5-year-olds.

Currently, the human resources department serves infants and toddlers in 75 of the state's 100 counties, mainly through multidisciplinary home teams that visit the families at least once a week. The goals now will be to get coverage of the remaining 25 counties and develop other models, particularly some that are based in centers, rather than the children's homes.

Washington Another possible solution to interagency strife is happening in Washington state, where Department of Education employee Susan Baxter, the state's early childhood interagency coordinator, spends her work day housed in the Department of Social and Health Services bridging what she calls a cross-cultural gap.

Baxter is responsible for bringing together the dozen state agencies that serve young handicapped children, as part of Washington's Birth to 6 State Planning Project. Her unusual office situation is part of an attempt to mend a rift that was created in 1983 after the state legislature passed a preschool mandate that in some instances caused existing programs to lose funding and new programs to be started in the school system, said Baxter, who's been in the early education field for 17 years.

"In some cases, that was devastating because existing programs had been in private nonprofit schools and the school districts may in some cases never have handled children under 5," said Baxter. "So it was a rough start, rough for families, rough for agencies that lost money, rough for schools. Instead of placing me in [the Department of] Education and causing further paranoia that schools are going after the babies," she was placed in the Department of Social and Health Services.

The widely varying structures of the two divisions, as in many states, caused misunderstandings. One obvious difference: Washington's superintendent of public instruction is an elected official (tenure: 18 years), while the governor appoints the secretary of health and social services (average tenure: two years). One of Baxter's roles was to become a student of the two systems, to learn how they were alike and how they were different.

"It was sort of like cultural anthropology, like learning two cultures," she said. Baxter began to interpret things for each agency, showing them the things they had in common. "People in each organization often think those in the other aren't like them, but in reality they often want the same results, though they go about it in different ways."

Baxter learned that words in each system in Washington state had different meanings, one "perfect example," she said, being the term case management. Within EPSDT (the Early Periodic Screening, Diagnosis and Treatment program), she said, case management tends to mean outreach, identifying and bringing in potential clients. In public health, case management is very expensive, including family assessment, information and home visits. In education, the term case management is not used, but often, Baxter said, the work educators do with families is the same thing.

"Our dream is to have this program administered by a collective, as opposed to a single system," said Baxter. "We recognize the need for a lead agency, but it's important that the lead agency has the capacity and the perspective to allow the management of the program to be done by a collection of staff people from different systems."

* * *

Many states won't be able to adopt the North Carolina or Washington state approach, and much concern exists over moving toddlers into the preschool program. Hinda Miller, of the Upper Darby, Pa., School District, is one of many educators who are concerned because states can include more children in the birth through 2 program than in the preschool program.

"When those children get to school we will wind up with a lot of due process hearings, a lot of controversy between special ed and parents," she said. "They'll come to us with an IFSP [individualized family service plan] . . . and I'm going to say, 'That's nice, honey, I'll see you when he's really special ed.' The parents will say, 'My God, he *is* special ed,' and we'll end up in due process. I'm terribly concerned," Miller said.

CEC sees having two separate systems or models for the birth through 2 and the 3 through 5 populations causing potential problems unless careful, coordinated planning takes place, said Weintraub. "If the eligible infant and toddler population is significantly larger than the eligible preschool population then schools will be faced with possibly having to tell parents that their 3-year-old child is no longer eligible," he said. "Secondly, if the scope of services required for infants and toddlers is significantly more extensive than for preschoolers," schools may have to tell parents when their child reaches age 3 they will no longer receive services.

CEC, said Weintraub, has long been committed to a unified delivery system under the responsibility of public education but "did not believe at this time that the federal government should require such an approach. We hope that states in their planning will give consideration to an educational delivery system down to birth or design appropriate strategies to smooth the transition from infant and toddler programs to preschool programs."

From Our Rolodex

Susan W. Baxter
Early Childhood Interagency
 Coordinator
Department of Social and Health
 Services
Division of Children and Family
 Services
Mail Stop OB-41
Olympia, Wash. 98504
(206)753-1233

Joan Turner Clary
Early Childhood Special Education
 Program Consultant
Iowa Department of Education
Grimes State Office Bldg.
Des Moines, Iowa 50319
(515)281-3176

Jonah M. Deppe
Coordinator
Early Intervention State Plan
Department of Special Education
 Services
100 N. First
Springfield, Ill. 62777
(217)782-6601

Duncan Munn
Chief of Day Services
Division of Mental Health and
 Mental Retardation
Albermarle Bldg.
325 N. Salisbury St.
Raleigh, N.C. 27611
(919)733-3654

Barbara J. Smith
Early Childhood Policy Consultant
19 Hartford St.
Pittsburgh, Pa. 15203
(412)431-3371

Phillip S. Strain
Director
The Early Childhood Research
    Institute
Western Psychiatric Institute
    and Clinic
3811 O'Hara St.
Pittsburgh, Pa. 15213
(412)624-2012

Frederick J. Weintraub
Assistant Executive Director
Council for Exceptional Children
1920 Association Dr.
Reston, Va. 22091
(703)620-3660

Karl R. White
Director
Early Intervention Effectiveness
    Institute
Exceptional Child Center
Utah State University, UMN 68
Logan, Utah 84322
(801)750-2029

Deborah Ziegler
Delaware Early Childhood
    Diagnostic and Intervention
    Center
Lake Forest South Elementary
Harrington, Del. 19952
(302)736-4557

Case Study 2.1

Program: AID, the Adolescent-Infant Development Program, Howard University Hospital, Washington, D.C.

Summary: The project trains 60 adolescent mothers of handicapped or at-risk infants and toddlers in the medical, educational, developmental, nutritional and safety needs of their children. It also provides intensive services for 20 of their children, from birth through age 2.

Contacts: 1. Eva Molnar, AID director, Department of Pediatrics and Child Health, Howard University Hospital, 2041 Georgia Ave. NW, Washington, D.C. 20060, (202)745-1596 or (202)636-5724
2. Roberta Clark, AID coordinator, Department of Pediatrics and Child Health, Howard University Hospital, 2041 Georgia Ave. NW, Washington, D.C. 20060, (202)745-1596

Babies born to adolescents are likely to have serious health and learning problems that will only get worse unless their mothers are trained to deal with them. And because the mothers are basically still children themselves, they'd have a hard time raising any baby, never mind trying to cope with a handicapped child.

The Adolescent-Infant Development (AID) Program at Howard University Hospital in Washington, D.C., is designed to teach adolescent mothers how to rear their handicapped children. And, more than that, it helps the teens take care of themselves, helping them stay in school, find jobs and arrange child care.

"We feel we have to meet the needs of the adolescents because if their needs are not met, we cannot meet the needs of the infant," said AID director Eva Molnar, who is also a clinical assistant professor of pediatrics at Howard's College of Medicine.

The program, which began in 1980 with a U.S. Education Department grant, specializes in girls age 15 and younger who are at risk of having a handicapped baby or who already have done so. Older adolescents are served under special circumstances, such as if they are expecting twins or have a severely handicapped baby. From the prenatal period through delivery and the child's first three years, AID staff members instruct and assist parents in the medical, educational, developmental, nutritional and safety needs of their children.

When an infant first comes to the program, either from Howard's intensive care nursery or referral by a local physician, Cassandra Williams takes over. The AID teacher and child development specialist assesses the child, using well-known instruments such as the Brazelton Neonatal Behavioral Assessment, and then develops education plans individually designed to meet the infant's needs.

During the child's first year of life, Williams and other AID staff members visit the child every six weeks to conduct 30- to 60-minute enrichment sessions.

Meanwhile, AID social worker Frances Alves starts to work on the adolescent mother. If the girl was referred to AID while she was pregnant, Alves already has worked with her, teaching her about changes in her body, the importance of good nutrition, and trying to keep her in school. After the baby is born, Alves works on proper mother-child bonding, training the girl in child development and parenting skills, helping her to get child care and stay in school, and teaching her how to prevent repeat pregnancies.

Alves considers it crucial that she and other AID staff stick with the new mother as the infant grows into a toddler, for several reasons. One reason, Alves said, is that a mother of a handicapped child "feels guilty taking time for herself. You have to tell her it's normal to set aside time for yourself." Alves will even help the mother find a babysitter to take care of the child for an hour or so.

Such feelings can lead to resentment of the child, and, often, child abuse, said Clark. "We give them alternatives. If you feel like hitting the baby when it's crying, put the baby in its room, close the door and ignore the crying. Or, call a neighbor."

And AID staff members work to avoid a common situation they believe contributes to repeat pregnancies: excessive attention to pregnant girls to the exclusion of parenting girls. Typically, "the only way to get attention and services is to get pregnant," said Clark. Instead, "we stand by you, get you back in school, link your handicapped child up with services that are available."

These case management services are critical for girls who tire of their baby after the initial flurry of attention, Clark added. "After the first year, that's the crucial point. The novelty of the new baby has worn off. The girl says, 'I've got myself together now. I'm in school, I'm in college. I don't want this baby.'"

AID's services are tailored to the mainly black community Howard University Hospital serves. While the hospital attracts patients from all over the world, AID by and large focuses on the neighborhoods around the hospital, which staff describe as the poorest in the

District of Columbia. Staff members need to be aware that the mother may have used drugs, or that, for example, PCP dust may be floating around the child's bedroom and getting into the child's skin, Molnar said.

"I'm not saying we're successful in dealing with all family problems. But you name it, we have it," said Molnar. "There are many contingencies that can arise. Where will the young woman stay? Many will say, 'I can't tell my mother because she'll put me out. She put my sister out.'"

In other cases, more than one sibling in the family is pregnant or parenting, said Clark. Sometimes, their mother may treat each girl differently. "One may be the black sheep or have a personality conflict with the mother. One may have a normal baby, the other may have a handicapped baby."

Community standards were part of the reason for dropping AID's former eligibility age limit of 19 to 15, said Molnar. "There is a dividing line in this community. Having a baby at age 16 is acceptable to some families, while having a baby at age 15 is not. So, socially it's not as acceptable, which affects family support and peer relationships. Of course we all know that with adolescents, a crucial factor if you're going to make it is family support."

Support for younger adolescents is also missing from other Washington, D.C., social agencies, which tend to focus on the high schools. "There is a big push against teen pregnancy in the D.C. high schools," said Clark. But little is done in the elementary schools or even the junior highs, she said.

"What do 12-year-olds in elementary school do, they have no programs," said Clark. And it's not unusual to have a pregnant girl in elementary school, said Williams. "In one elementary school, they commented they'd never had a class of sixth graders without a pregnant girl," Williams said. "So the question becomes, who's going to make it to high school first, the girl or her baby?"

There are also physiological reasons for the program to focus on the younger girls, said Molnar. "Adolescents 15 and under are different than 16 to 19 year olds. They can exhibit physical immaturity, mental instability," she said.

And girls in middle adolescence — ages 13 to the 16th birthday — are just beginning the normal breaking away from the family when pregnancy interrupts. "The adolescent is just beginning to become independent," said Clark. "With the birth of the baby she becomes dependent again."

Her renewed dependence, coupled with an extra child in the house, may cause resentment among other family members who have to make a sacrifice for the baby, Clark added. "It's possible the sibling will be displaced because the girl [with the baby] needs a bigger bedroom. It also affects the social life of the family — the grandmother may need to babysit," she said.

The AID staff is aware that their advice may cause arguments within the family. Their lessons on childrearing may differ from the way the girl's mother believes in raising children. "We don't want to cause any more division, friction in the family," Clark said.

Having a handicapped baby heightens the problems pregnant or parenting teens typically have in maintaining a relationship with the baby's father, Williams said. "A handicapped baby can split a family even with stable adults. There is a high rate of divorce in families with handicapped children," she said. "With an adolescent whose relationship is already unstable and shaky, it's even more difficult."

Molnar, Clark, Alves and Williams all said they had never seen an adolescent relationship survive where the baby is born handicapped. "In this community, young men are proud to father a child," said Molnar. And not to father a "normal" child, added Clark, is "devastating."

The father will blame the baby's handicap on the mother and try to father another child with a different partner, said Williams. The girl will also want another baby so she's at risk for another pregnancy, added Alves. She's also at risk for suicide.

"The girl will have feelings of guilt and shame because the baby is handicapped," said Clark. "They think, 'I should have waited.'"

By keeping an eye on the girls through their child's third birthday, the AID staff is able to minimize many of the problems the mothers go through.

"I think everyone has been convinced now," of the program's effectiveness, said Molnar. Howard University Hospital now funds the program, whose federal grant ran out in 1986. "This hospital has been ahead of legal developments in providing services, first to infants, second to adolescents," she said.

Chapter Three

Three Through Five: Challenges In Serving Preschoolers

The new preschool program poses a dual problem for states. They must fulfill an entitlement to serve all handicapped preschoolers by 1991 or risk losing a portion of their federal funding. They also must place these children in the least restrictive educational environment, with few options for integrating handicapped and nonhandicapped children in the classroom.

Until recently, the U.S. Education Department has not enforced classroom integration of handicapped preschoolers with their nonhandicapped peers, although it is required under the 1975 Education for All Handicapped Children Act, P.L. 94-142. Under P.L. 94-142, states that voluntarily serve handicapped preschoolers have had a mandate to provide 3- through 5-year-olds with the same "least restrictive environment" placement as they offer school-age handicapped children.

The federal government for more than 10 years has judged preschool programs' compliance loosely because, unlike school-age programs, preschool programs for nonhandicapped children are not mandated by any state, a policy gap that severely limits the number of classrooms available for integration.

Robert Black, state special education director for South Carolina, said when his state applied for preschool incentive grant funds in 1978, "We were told by the feds that for 3- to 4-year-olds, least restrictive environment did not apply" because there were no public preschool programs for nonhandicapped children in the state.

But under the 1986 amendments to the Education of the Handicapped Act, P.L. 99-457, least restrictive environment—often referred to as mainstreaming—has become "the dead center issue," Black said, leaving questions about how far states must go to integrate handicapped and nonhandicapped preschoolers.

It is unclear whether the federal government will strictly enforce the provision. Least restrictive environment "was not the driving issue" in designing P.L. 99-457, according to Gray Garwood, staff director for the House Select Education Subcommittee during the development of the law. "The driving issue is to make services available to all 3- to 5-year-olds. To the extent that [least restrictive environment] is possible, that's great. But some states don't have public educational classrooms for 3-year-olds," said Garwood, who now is staff director for the House Postsecondary Education Subcommittee.

But in cases where integration is appropriate, schools should not place handicapped children in separate classrooms out of convenience, he added.

Lisbeth Vincent, president of the Council for Exceptional Children's Division for Early Childhood, agreed convenience should not be the deciding factor. The handicapped preschooler's socialization needs must come first, said Vincent, who also is a professor of rehabilitation psychology and special education at the University of Wisconsin.

Judging from the last decade of research, "It's pretty clear that a large number [of handicapped preschoolers] make as good progress, and in some cases better, when served in settings that include their [nonhandicapped] peers," Vincent said.

* * *

States have limited options for establishing least restrictive environment. Handicapped children can be served in a variety of programs, including public preschools, Head Start, child care centers and private preschools. But because these programs are administered by different agencies and operate under different standards, integration can be an administrative nightmare.

Integration is not very popular with schools, according to Gloria Harbin, associate director of state policies for the State Technical Assistance Resource Team (START) program at the University of North Carolina's Frank Porter Graham Child Development Center in Chapel Hill. Schools "have to go through a lot of contortions to integrate children. Because it's difficult, people don't do it very often," she said.

Although schools have had little success in integrating preschool classrooms, they are basically the only other place besides Head Start where integration is even a possibility.

"Education-supported programs for [handicapped] preschoolers have historically been a real small piece of the pie," said Phillip S. Strain, director of the University of Pittsburgh's Early Childhood Research Institute. State mental health and mental retardation agencies and private service providers "have really dominated the [preschool] field and they're not subject to anything remotely resembling" least restrictive environment, he said.

On the bright side, Strain said, P.L. 99-457 may create more integration opportunities simply by funding more school-based programs that can provide a least restrictive environment.

The Head Start Option

Head Start programs have far more experience than the public schools in integrating and serving handicapped preschoolers. Since 1973 Head Start programs have had a federal mandate to reserve at least 10 percent of their enrollment for handicapped preschoolers. Because of Head Start's longstanding presence in the community, schools often view the programs as the most convenient vehicle for integration.

P.L. 99-457 follows Head Start as the second federal program to require services for handicapped preschoolers. Because these two programs are set up to serve many of the same children, their administrative goals are prone to conflict.

In some cases, Head Start and the public schools fight to serve the same handicapped children to meet their classroom quotas for receiving federal and state funds. In other instances, public schools refer handicapped preschoolers to Head Start to save themselves the expense of serving the children.

The degree of cooperation between Head Start and public schools differs from state to state and from community to community. The questions of which program should serve the child, and, in the case of joint services, which program should pay for which services, are the issues that draw the most controversy.

The state education departments of New Jersey and Louisiana won't contract with Head Start to provide handicapped preschoolers with special education services. Both states say Head Start doesn't meet the standards of an approved education program and therefore is not eligible for state special education funds. "If a kid is in a day care surrounding, that's not an educational environment," said Jeffrey Osowski, New Jersey's special education director.

Neither will New Jersey integrate children into Head Start full time because it can't ensure program quality, said Osowski. Occasionally, however, a New Jersey public school will send a handicapped child to Head Start two days a week for a social experience. In these cases, the school pays for the child's related health services without paying Head Start tuition.

In Louisiana, Head Start programs can accept handicapped children referred by the public schools, but, as in New Jersey, they are not reimbursed for daily tuition. "Our money can't flow to Head Starts and day care centers; they don't meet regular educational requirements," said Taran Tucker, education consultant for the Louisiana Education Department's Division of Special Education.

Louisiana schools that refer handicapped children to Head Start programs send special education teachers to visit the children in the programs and pay for any health services not defined as educational.

* * *

Massachusetts has sidestepped teacher and program certification problems similar to those that keep Louisiana and New Jersey from contracting with Head Start. The state education department relaxed its rule requiring Head Start programs to have certified special education teachers in every classroom and let special educators supervise Head Start teachers, many of whom have no teaching credentials.

The state let Head Start programs count their handicap service coordinator, who works with outside professionals and other agencies, as their special educator, according to Joanne Brady, director of Head Start's Region I Resource Access Project (RAP). RAP staff in each of Head Start's 10 administrative regions coordinate enrollment of handicapped children with state social service agencies. Each Head Start program has a handicap service coordinator, Brady said, and most are certified in special education.

Brady's staff negotiated the substitution of handicap service coordinators for special educators through a state interagency agreement between the Administration for Children, Youth and Families (ACYF)—the division of the U.S. Health and Human Services Department that administers Head Start—and the Massachusetts education department. Forty-two states have interagency agreements between Head Start and public schools to serve handicapped children, and RAPS have been responsible for negotiating most of the agreements, according to ACYF.

The Massachusetts interagency agreement calls for public schools, in most cases, to pay for serving the children it refers to Head Start after Head Start funds for handicapped children have run out. This helps Head Start serve its 10 percent quota of handicapped children without requesting extra federal funds for additional services.

The Head Start subsidy for serving handicapped children is modest, and many times cannot cover the cost of expensive therapy, said Brady.

Using Head Start as an integration option also can relieve public schools from the responsibility and cost of educating some handicapped preschoolers. Schools in Massachusetts pay Head Start tuition for the handicapped children they refer for full-time placement, Brady said, only when a Head Start program cannot afford to serve another child unless the school foots the bill.

The agreement works if both sides cooperate. But in some cases, said Brady, public schools pad enrollment in their special education preschool classes by keeping in segregated classrooms children that could be referred to Head Start. Referral would represent an extra cost to the school, she said, and when special education enrollment is low, extra children help pay for classroom staff.

Another problem reported in Massachusetts and other states is that schools may refuse to serve children Head Start refers to them for special education services because the children don't meet the schools' definition of handicapped. As a result, Brady said, Head Start spends too much of its money on serving mildly to moderately handicapped children.

"Head Start is spending more of their money on language and occupational therapy and even, in some cases, physical therapy service," said Anne Lynch, president of the Massachusetts Head Start Association. "We're sometimes between a rock and a hard place. If the school system doesn't see the child as handicapped, what are we going to do, not serve the child?" Lynch says her program's enrollment of handicapped children is between 25 percent and 35 percent, well over the 10 percent minimum.

* * *

Some Head Start programs view P.L. 99-457 as a threat to their ability to fill their 10 percent minimum enrollment of handicapped children, said Carillon Olmsted, RAP director of training in Head Start's Region X, which serves Washington, Oregon, Idaho and Alaska.

To fight the perceived threat, Olmsted said, Head Start programs in her region have become their own advocates, trying to sell the benefits of their services to the public schools.

In the past, Head Start has been a major identifier of Washington state's handicapped children, she said. Now Washington Head Start programs "have to work harder to make districts see they're a good place to mainstream kids." Head Start programs also try to sell schools on their parent support services, Olmsted said, which schools traditionally don't provide.

In Pennsylvania, the state Office of Mental Retardation has for 10 years subsidized Head Start's integration efforts. Funds provided under P.L. 94-142 go to Head Start programs through local education agencies and intermediate units that have "traditionally wanted nothing to do with us," said Sharon Jones, president of the Pennsylvania Head Start Association.

Head Start programs in Pennsylvania fear the public schools will shut them out of serving handicapped children by setting standards for integration — such as requiring all Head Start instructors to have education degrees — that are too high for the programs to meet, Jones said.

The question of standards applies to Head Start's funding as well, Jones said. Pennsylvania's programs won't be able to take handicapped children referred by the public schools unless the schools pay for the child's Head Start slot, which they may not do if Head Start can't qualify as an educational program. "None of our Head Starts can afford it if we don't get money for our basic educational program," she said.

* * *

Clennie Murphy, chief of ACYF's Head Start bureau, warns Head Start programs not to take on too many handicapped students because special services drain funds and dilute program quality. When Head Start programs exhaust their funds for special services, they must request more money from their regional office. Additional funds would have to come from a region's discretionary account, which is used to enhance program quality throughout the region.

"The philosophy in Head Start is only to take on what we can handle. We're not going to take kids in the program if we can't serve them well," said Murphy.

"Here's our concern: public schools should serve all handicapped kids that are eligible, not just those kids from advantaged families," Murphy said. A disadvantaged family with a handicapped child should understand that if a Head Start program is full, they can turn to the public schools, he said.

Not all children in Head Start programs are disadvantaged; up to 10 percent of all Head Start children may exceed its low-income guidelines.

* * *

Payor Of Last Resort It's unclear whether public schools or Head Start programs must ultimately pay for services to handicapped preschoolers. The law includes a "payor of last resort" clause similar to one included in Head Start's authorization. The duplication makes both the federal departments of education and health and human services responsible for the costs of services for handicapped preschoolers if other agencies refuse to pay.

"There is a conflict, that much we know, and it's up to the states and the federal government to work that out," said congressional aide Gray Garwood.

But striking a compromise between the two departments won't be easy, he said. Health and Human Services "is much happier if Education is the payor of last resort." The Education Department would, however, be amenable to an agreement, Garwood said.

Frederick Weintraub, assistant executive director of the Council for Exceptional Children (CEC), also recognized the discrepancy. "Part of the problem is a failure of the federal agencies to get their act together," he said. The federal government encourages states to form interagency agreements when it won't do so itself, Weintraub said.

Turning The Tables On Integration

Head Start is not the only option open to public schools trying to place handicapped preschoolers in the least restrictive environment. Reverse integration is another possibility. Using this approach, schools bring two or three nonhandicapped children into their special education classrooms.

CEC's Vincent is preparing a grant proposal for the U.S. Education Department that will explore the possibilities of reverse integration. The model benefits staff who won't have to travel to serve handicapped preschoolers integrated in regular preschools in the community, she said.

The reverse integration approach has been in practice since 1980 in New York's North Syracuse Central School District. The district places one or two nonhandicapped children, with their parents' permission, in classrooms with severely multiply handicapped preschoolers, according to Warren Grund, district assistant superintendent for special education. Like the handicapped students, the nonhandicapped children attend the program five days a week, from 9 a.m. to 2 p.m.

The program is not so much an educational as a socializing experience for the nonhandicapped children, said Grund, and their response to the experience is heartwarming. After a short while in the classroom, the nonhandicapped children try to teach the handicapped children. "The [nonhandicapped] kids just get in there. They're not afraid, they're sensitized to the situation" before they enter the class, he said.

From this experience, strong friendship bonds develop between the handicapped and nonhandicapped children, Grund said. "These kids become advocates for the handicapped kids when they get into kindergarten and first grade."

Grund also said the response from parents of nonhandicapped children in the community is tremendous. The school has received 400 to 500 calls since advertising the program in local newspapers. "We don't give parents enough credit. They want their kids to grow up in a society that understands the handicapped. They want their kids to get along with everybody," he said.

Parents of nonhandicapped children don't pay tuition, but they do cover the cost of extra activities, such as paying for transportation if the class goes on a field trip, he said.

A drawback of this integration model is that so few nonhandicapped children can be placed in the special education classrooms. Syracuse limits the number "to a level where the [nonhandicapped] kids are assets to the overall program and not detracting from teacher time available to each individual child," said Kathleen Esposito, principal of Main Street Elementary School, where the program is housed.

Another problem with using the reverse integration model for P.L. 99-457 programs is that federal law precludes special education funds from serving nonhandicapped children. Syracuse has avoided the issue, Grund said, because the program receives its support from the state.

Other communities also are using the reverse integration model, sometimes with support from state mental retardation agencies. One state special education director, who asked not to be identified, said her state was using this approach with public education funds, adding that no one has ever opposed the practice.

* * *

Another integration model would coordinate public school services with child care centers, Vincent said. Using one approach, a public school would offer a child care program space in its building at a below-market rent. In exchange, the child care center would free up five slots in the program for the school's handicapped children. The school would supply the center with support and supervisory staff, Vincent said.

But because enrollment for grades one through six has escalated nationwide in recent years, classroom space may not be available in elementary schools, she said. While a similar situation, of course, will soon follow in the upper grades, high schools currently are experiencing a decline. Vincent suggested child care centers look for open spaces in public high schools. High school placement has benefits, she said. High school students could work as aides in the child care programs and possibly develop an interest in the special education profession. One district with this kind of program in its high school is Pinellas County, Fla. (see Case Study 3.2).

As a side benefit, Vincent said, high school girls working in the program may be deterred from becoming teenage mothers after seeing how difficult it is to take care of children, handicapped or nonhandicapped.

Schools also could integrate handicapped children into community child care centers by placing special educators in the programs, she said. This approach has both benefits and drawbacks. Handicapped children probably would receive more education in a public school classroom using the reverse model, Vincent said. But a handicapped child placed in a community child care center would tend to develop friendships with nonhandicapped children that are likely to continue through the early elementary school grades. "That's critical for kids," she said.

California's state education department places some handicapped children in child care centers and serves children already enrolled in centers that are later identified as handicapped. Handicapped children attend the centers for part of the day, often accompanied by their special education aides or teachers.

The public schools pay for the accompanying staff and transportation to and from the centers, but parents are responsible for child care tuition, according to Nancy Obley-Kilborn, manager of the California education department's infant-preschool unit.

In other states, opportunities to integrate children into child care centers often depend on the centers' interest and ability to accept the child. Training child care staff to work with handicapped children is one option discussed in Chapter Five.

Public School Options

Integrating handicapped children into state-funded prekindergarten programs is another way to provide the least restrictive environment. As more states create and operate such programs in public schools, the possibilities expand. But because most of these programs are designed to serve low-income and disadvantaged preschoolers, states face the question of what constitutes pure integration.

About 20 states have started to develop networks of early childhood programs run by the public schools. And many of them have visions of eventually expanding their programs to serve all preschoolers.

But in the short term, most of these programs are set up to serve preschoolers who benefit most from developmental services, children who either are poor or at risk of academic failure because they suffer from developmental delays, speak no English or come from difficult family situations.

In many of the states that offer public preschool programs, the schools are allowed, and sometimes encouraged, to contract with outside agencies to run the programs. Public schools can turn to Head Start programs, nonprofit child care centers or, in a few cases, private for-profit early childhood programs.

The idea of state-funded preschools is a relatively new one, becoming popular only in the 1980s. Most public preschool systems still are not widespread within their states and may not be available to coordinate with special education programs.

Some experts believe it is inappropriate to place handicapped children in at-risk preschool programs. Agreeing with this view is Edith Helmich, a research scientist for the Illinois state board of education.

"Putting a handicapped child in this situation might defeat both purposes," Helmich said. The disadvantaged children her program serves need the same amount of attention and individualization handicapped children would, she said. "In this program, [integration] really should not be happening." Illinois' at-risk program, started in 1985, operates in 100 of the state's 1,000 school districts.

South Carolina is working on a strategy to mix preschool special education services with its existing program for at-risk preschoolers. Using P.L. 99-457 funds, the state would hire special education consultants to work with preschool teachers. The consultants would help the teachers develop appropriate individualized education programs (IEP) for children enrolled in the at-risk program who are later identified as handicapped.

Assuming that South Carolina mandates services for 3- through 5-year-olds, State Special Education Director Robert Black said the plan would be fine, with one stipulation. The local education agency—which would be responsible for serving all handicapped children, even if they are identified within the at-risk program— would have to be sure that placing the children in the at-risk program outweighs the benefits of placing them with nonhandicapped children of more diverse backgrounds.

Keeping handicapped disadvantaged preschoolers in the at-risk program cannot be done "out of convenience," Black said. "If you have an at-risk program, that's hardly a least restrictive environment. . . . Those kids are at risk, therefore, those kids are handicapped or darn close to being handicapped."

Is the grouping of handicapped children with low-income and other disadvantaged children a true integration experience? "I've never seen any research to support that social interaction can only be effective if it's mixed across classes," said Garwood. "These low-income programs, they may have cheaper toys," but sharing among the children still goes on, he said.

Susan Baxter, Washington state's early childhood interagency coordinator, opposes integrating handicapped preschoolers with low-income children. "It further reinforces the caste system. We're sending a message to society about being different," she said.

Baxter said many parents of handicapped children favor integration because they want nonhandicapped children to form emotional bonds with their children and learn to see beyond their impairments. These nonhandicapped children later can become advocates for handicapped individuals when they mature and become our nation's decisionmakers, she said.

Middle class children can face fewer obstacles than disadvantaged youngsters to assuming influential roles in society. Yet the structure of our education delivery system makes it difficult to pay for the mixing of nonhandicapped middle-class preschoolers with their handicapped peers.

Public schools can contract for services with private preschools and child care centers, but often are discouraged by the high price tag that private school programs carry.

The most cost-effective options for integration appear to be those that perpetuate class segregation: placing handicapped preschoolers in Head Start or sending them to federally subsidized child care programs for low-income families or other public child care centers that serve primarily low-income children.

If public schools choose to work with the more expensive private preschools or child care centers, they could choose to absorb the extra costs or pass them on to parents.

Approaches such as Vincent's recommendation to offer child care centers low rent in public schools or North Syracuse's reverse integration model that serves children of all income brackets are possible solutions to breaking down class barriers.

Funding Questions

Funding programs that try to place handicapped preschoolers in the least restrictive environment can be as difficult a task as coordinating them. The question is, will Congress continue to back up with appropriations the preschool programs it has authorized? And if it doesn't, how will states pick up the slack?

As discussed in Chapter One, many education leaders never meant for states to provide as much of the funding as they have for school-age handicapped children—91 percent of the share—and resent the prospect of fully subsidizing services for preschoolers.

By creating a special education entitlement for 3- through 5-year-olds, "Congress created a civil right to service," said Nicholas Penning, legislative specialist with the American Association for School Administrators (AASA). States will have no choice but to provide preschool programs, no matter what the cost. "You'll be taken to court if you don't serve handicapped kids," he said.

Many states that provide preschool special education under P.L. 94-142 have found it necessary, in an attempt to maintain a balance of services across district lines, to supplement programs in less wealthy communities with state funds.

Michigan was one such state until the automobile industry hit hard times in 1982. When the state's economic growth slowed, schools found it difficult to fund their entitlement program for 3- through 5-year-olds. "We lost a lot of education funding, we lost state funding," said Edward Birch, Michigan's special education director. Schools "have had to make up much of that revenue through programs that would have gone to general education."

* * *

Other states are in happier circumstances and already are planning how they will use their extra federal funds. In Rhode Island, which mandates services to handicapped children from age 3, State Special Education Director Robert Pryhoda would like to expand such related services for preschoolers as speech, occupational and physical therapy.

He also wants to expand family services. "We traditionally concentrate on the child," he said. With the help of P.L. 99-457 funds, Rhode Island will be "giving more programming to the parents and assisting them a lot" with case managers.

States that must build preschool services from scratch are in the planning process. North Carolina's education department has drafted two proposals to help finance the new entitlement program. The department will recommend first that the state legislature give schools $2,000 for every child they already serve and $1,000 for each new child they serve. This will balance the funds the federal government will give schools for serving new children. The proposal would cost the state $3.4 million.

Under the alternative plan, the legislature would gradually phase in model programs until each of the state's 140 school districts had one (50 districts in North Carolina already operate such programs). The model programs would be funded totally from state and federal dollars, placing no financial burden on the communities, according to Janis Dellinger, an analyst with the state education department's division for exceptional children.

* * *

As states grapple with funding issues, they also must untangle the web of regulations that stymie integration: certification requirements that only allow special education certified teachers to work with handicapped children, and special education dollars that can only be spent on programs that are purely instructional. Perhaps some states will have to redefine "educational experience" to facilitate integration.

Public schools must learn to work with Head Starts, child care centers and other facilities that serve nonhandicapped children to negotiate a smooth strategy for integration. State and local interagency councils are the first step to working out agreements between various early childhood programs. This process will require much fine tuning, perhaps some rewriting of regulations and an altruistic effort to forego the convenience of segregation for the benefit of the children P.L. 99-457 was designed to serve.

From Our Rolodex

Robert Black
Director of Special Education
South Carolina Department of Education
1429 Senate St.
Columbia, S.C. 29201
(803)758-3291

Janis Dellinger
Division for Exceptional Children
North Carolina Department of Education
116 W. Edenton St.
Raleigh, N.C. 27603
(919)733-6081

Warren Grund
Assistant Superintendent for Special Education and Pupil-Personnel Services
North Syracuse Central School District
5355 W. Taft Road
North Syracuse, N.Y. 13212
(315)470-3204

Nancy Obley-Kilborn
Infant-Preschool Unit Manager
Special Education Division
California Department of Education
721 Capitol Mall
Sacramento, Calif. 95814
(916)324-8417

Lisbeth Vincent
Professor of Rehabilitation
 Psychology and Special Education
University of Wisconsin
432 N. Murray
Madison, Wis. 53706
(608)263-5824

*Head Start Resource Access
 Project Directors*

Region I—Connecticut, Maine,
 Massachusetts, New Hampshire,
 Rhode Island, Vermont
Joanne P. Brady
Director
New England RAP
Education Development Center, Inc.
55 Chapel St.
Newton, Mass. 02160
(617)969-7100

Region II—New York, New Jersey,
 Puerto Rico, Virgin Islands
Dinah Heller
Director
New York University RAP
School of Continuing Education
48 Cooper Square
Room 103
New York, N.Y. 10003
(212)477-9120

Region III—Delaware, Maryland,
 Pennsylvania, Virginia,
 Washington, D.C., West Virginia
JoAn Herren
Director
University of Maryland RAP
Head Start Resource and Training
 Center
4321 Hartwick Rd., L-220
College Park, Md. 20740
(301)454-5786

Region IV—Florida, Georgia,
 North Carolina, South Carolina,
 Alabama, Kentucky, Tennessee
Anne Sanford
Director
Chapel Hill RAP
Chapel Hill Training-
 Outreach Project
Lincoln Center, Merrill Mill Road
Chapel Hill, N.C. 27514
(919)967-8295

Anne Sanford
Project Director
Mississippi RAP
Friends of Children of
 Mississippi, Inc.
119 Mayes St.
Jackson, Miss. 39213
(601)362-9154

Region V—Illinois, Indiana, Ohio,
 Michigan, Minnesota, Wisconsin
Merie B. Karnes
Director
Great Lakes RAP
Colonel Wolfe School
403 East Healey
Champaign, Ill. 61820
(217)333-3876

Region VI—Arkansas, Louisiana,
 New Mexico, Oklahoma, Texas
Mary Tom Riley
Director
Texas Tech University RAP
P.O. Box 4170
Lubbock, Texas 79409
(806)742-3296

Region VII-Iowa, Kansas, Missouri,
 Nebraska
Richard Whelan
Director
Region VII Head Start RAP
CRU 26
University of Kansas Medical Center
Kansas City, Kan. 66103
(913)588-5961

Three Through Five

Region VIII — Colorado, Montana, North Dakota, South Dakota, Utah, Wyoming
Jane Amundson
Director
The Denver RAP
Greenlee Metro Lab School
Metropolitan State College
1150 Lipan Street, Room 105
Denver, Colo. 80204
(303)571-1824

Region IX-Arizona, California, Nevada, Guam, Hawaii, American Samoa
Ginger Mach-Ward
Project Director
Southwest Human Development RAP
Suite 302
3008 N. Third St.
Phoenix, Ariz. 85012
(602)266-5976

Region X — Idaho, Oregon, Washington, Alaska
Carillon Olmsted
Director of Training
Region X Rap
Portland State University
P.O. Box 1491
Portland, Ore. 97207
(503)229-4815

Antonia Dobrec
Project Director
Indian RAP
Three Feather Associates
P.O. Box 5508
Norman, Okla. 73070
(405)360-2919

Case Study 3.1

Program: Project STEPS, Sequenced Transition to Education in the Public Schools

Summary: The program is designed to help handicapped children move from preschool to the least restrictive environment in the public schools. The project serves children from birth to age 5 with follow-up services for children age 6 who have entered the public schools. The focus is on children in the year prior to their transition to the public schools.

Contacts: 1. Peggy Stephens, executive director, Child Development Centers of the Bluegrass, Inc., 465 Springhill Dr., Lexington, Ky. 40503, (606)278-0549
2. Norman D. Osborne, assistant superintendent, Fayette County Public Schools, Lexington, Ky. 40502, (606)259-1411
3. Mark Wolery, associate professor, Department of Special Education, University of Kentucky, Lexington, Ky. 40506, (606)257-7929
4. Linda Dyk, director, Cardinal Hill Hospital Preschool, 2050 Versailles Road, Lexington, Ky. 40504, (606)254-5701

In 1982, the relationship between the Fayette County Public Schools and the local private preschools could not have been worse.

"We hated each other," said Peggy Stephens, executive director of the Child Development Centers of the Bluegrass, Inc. "Hate is a mild description."

"I'd call it an atmosphere of mutual distrust," agreed Norman Osborne, assistant superintendent of the Fayette County Public Schools. "I remember the first time I went to a meeting with a group of parents. You could just feel it in the atmosphere."

One of the local preschools, located at Cardinal Hill Hospital in Lexington, was embroiled in a due process hearing over a handicapped preschooler's transition to the public schools. The hearing "had gotten really nasty. There was a lot of bad blood," said Mark Wolery, an associate professor at the University of Kentucky. Agreed Stephens: "We were really aggravated with the public schools. There was a real 'us, them' mentality."

Something had to be done. So Stephens got together with Linda

Dyk, director of the Cardinal Hill Preschool, and Ellen Perry, director of the Growing Together Preschool, Inc., and formed the Preschool Interagency Planning Council (PIPC). One of its goals: to improve handicapped children's transition from preschool to the public schools.

The preschool directors thought the due process hearing had resulted from "a lack of understanding. Both the public school system and the preschool system did not know enough about each other," said Dyk.

So PIPC applied for — and got — a three-year U.S. Education Department grant to develop a transition program. The Fayette schools signed on as a participant in the project, known as STEPS, or Sequenced Transition to Education in the Public Schools.

Now happily ensconced in the third year of the grant, all parties are quick to reveal their former mutual antipathy, and even quicker to illustrate how dramatically things have changed.

The preschool programs "had really provided a close-knit parent group, a very sheltered kind of experience" for handicapped children, Osborne said. "Parents were very fearful about their [children's] entrance into public school, what services would be provided, whether or not they'd be treated honestly and fairly."

Through the transition program, "we've been able to turn that whole thing around, make a very smooth transition," he said. "Parents are very pleased with our end results and the cooperative efforts that take place."

Dyk said STEPS has caused a reduction in the number of the preschool parents' complaints about the public schools. In fact, Dyk said, no parents of former Cardinal Hill students have complained about the appropriateness of their handicapped child's placement in the public schools; instead, she now gets just relatively minor complaints about things they can work out, such as transportation.

How does the program work?

The first of four prongs is an administrative structure that lets preschools negotiate administrative issues, such as transfer of records and preplacement assessments, with the public schools. Second, preschool staff are taught how public schools are set up and funded, while public school staff learn how to work with incoming students and their parents. As part of the training, the staff members visit each others' schools, attend workshops and view videotapes.

STEPS' third prong focuses on parents of handicapped children, who learn how to prepare for their child's entrance into the public schools. It's a weaning process, getting parents to become more independent. "We empower parents, not do everything for them, because we won't always be there for them," said Stephens. Preschool staff learn to deal with parents' compliments properly. Parents will say, "'We just love you, no one else will be as good a teacher as you've been to my child.' We say we appreciate that, but trust us, they're good too," she said.

And preschool staff are trained to deal with the inevitable calls from parents with problems. "We tell them [staff members], 'Be careful when that parent calls you with a problem that you realize you're hearing only one side.' Our role is to be as supportive as possible, but also as objective as possible," Stephens said.

Public school staff, meanwhile, are trained to work with parents and preschools as partners in a joint endeavor, said Osborne. Initially, staff members conduct question and answer sessions with parents, letting them know what kinds of programs are available in the public schools. Later, he said, they work in cooperation with parents to make placement decisions for their children.

STEPS teaches parents how to prepare for the IEP (individualized education program) meetings, where placement decisions are made. "We try to structure the IEP committee meeting as much as possible by setting up an agenda to involve parent participation," said Stephens. "We have the parent and preschool develop specific recommendations for the IEP. We start the meeting with them presenting, kind of: 'Hi, we'd like to introduce this child to you.'"

At Glendover Elementary School, parents attend slide presentations where teachers talk about what their school is all about, from the regular kindergarten and first grades to the schools' four classrooms for severely handicapped children. Preschool parents also periodically visit the school and observe classrooms in action, said Principal Jana Fremd.

Fremd believes parents are convinced the public schools are looking out for the best interests of their children. "Some of the parents who were the most outspoken, most resistant, who were sure their children were going to be mistreated, they are now our best advocates," she said. "They've seen what changes have occurred and what improvements their children have made."

The fourth and final prong, of course, is training the students themselves. Going through a lunch line and finding your way around a building may not seem difficult, but to handicapped preschoolers used to being escorted to and from a bus, it can be next to impossible.

Those basic kinds of functional skills are now taught in the year before a preschooler is ready for public school. And the preschools are trying to loosen their protective shield around handicapped students as much as possible.

The public schools and preschools have come up with an Entry

Level Skills Checklist (see Appendix D) that teachers can complete in 10 minutes. It pinpoints specific skills, such as standing in line and eating lunch with little help, that children need to make a successful transition to the public schools.

For instance, students accustomed to preschool classes with 12 students and three staff members are "going to have difficulty surviving in a kindergarten with 25 children," said Stephens. "They may not understand that when they complete a task they are to complete it without teacher participation. That they are to raise their hand when completed and wait quietly or in a designated area, whatever is appropriate."

And handicapped students' IEPs pinpoint and target specific skills, so the IEP, particularly in the last year of preschool, becomes the transition plan.

Some of these skills are things that "could drive a kindergarten teacher up the wall," Stephens said. "Sometimes they [handicapped students] may be able to perform the skills, but they don't have the behavior."

The beauty of the STEPS program is that it can be easily replicated in other communities, according to Wolery, who said that unlike many early childhood projects, this one does not rely on particular teaching styles or personalities.

Instead, it involves systemic changes in the administration of programs that make it hard to observe but easy to implement. In fact, because the program was started in an atmosphere of "bad blood" and was successful anyway, its prospects elsewhere are even brighter, said Wolery, who is the project evaluator for STEPS.

"This project has been successful despite being implemented in a very bad context. That's what makes me fairly confident about it being replicable. It worked in a bad situation, so in a moderate to pleasant situation it would work very well," he said.

In addition, STEPS is a comprehensive model, as it addresses both parents and children as well as the communication between the preschool and public school programs, he said.

The Early Skills Entry Checklist by itself is so useful that school districts unable to adopt the complete STEPS program could use just the checklist, suggested Wolery.

Also easily replicable, said Stephens, is the PIPC concept of a grassroots organization of preschools. Her original three-preschool PIPC now is made up of seven preschools and the public schools, as well as a few affiliate members such as a representative from their regional mental health and mental retardation board. Stephens has helped 13 others spring up around Kentucky and neighboring Indiana communities and is in the process of setting up a fourteenth.

Besides Fayette County, four other central Kentucky counties have tried STEPS. "That's the beauty of it," said Wolery. "We know it can work in small rural districts and we know it can work in districts that serve a community of 220,000. We don't know about a large urban district like [Washington] D.C. or Chicago. I don't see why it wouldn't, but I would hate to say it does."

The next phase, if STEPS staff get the funds for which they have applied, is to replicate the program in three more sites, two in far western Kentucky and one in northern Kentucky. After that, possibly, statewide implementation, said Stephens.

For now, those in Fayette County will continue to refine STEPS, but the basic model is intact and working smoothly.

"I just couldn't be happier with the outcome of the whole thing," said Osborne. "We're just delighted with it." Fremd put it simply: "STEPS is working."

Case Study 3.2

Program: The High School/Preschool Partnership Program, Pinellas County, Fla.

Summary: The program, located in a high school, is designed to boost high school students' interest in special education and child care careers while providing educational child care to children. Students enrolled in a home economics child care program assist teachers and a teacher's aide in a class that serves 10 mildly to moderately handicapped children and 20 nonhandicapped children ages 3 through 5.

Contacts: **1.** Jonathan McIntire, supervisor, Low Prevalence Programs, Pinellas County Board of Education, 1895 Gulf-To-Bay Blvd., Clearwater, Fla. 33575, (813)442-1171
2. Sandra Broida, supervisor, Child Find, Florida Diagnostic and Learning Resource System, 1895 Gulf-To-Bay Blvd., Clearwater, Fla. 33575, (813)462-9687
3. Wendy Swertfeger, teacher, Varying Exceptionalities Pre-Kindergarten Program, High School/Preschool Partnership Program, Countryside High School, 3000 S.R. 580, Clearwater, Fla. 33519, (813)799-1100
4. Ruth Henderson, Home Economics Child Care teacher, High School/Preschool Partnership Program, Countryside High School, 3000 S.R. 580, Clearwater, Fla. 33519, (813)799-1100

Six years ago officials of the Pinellas County, Fla., School System investigated educational opportunities for moderately handicapped preschoolers in the district and found none.

"Through Child Find we kept locating youngsters who were mild to moderately handicapped who were not getting any pre-kindergarten program," said Sandra Broida, supervisor of the Pinellas County Child Find, which is a program required under the Education for All Handicapped Children Act to identify, locate and evaluate all handicapped children. The state of Florida does not require schools to provide preschool special education programs.

"These were children with speech and language problems, hearing and visually impaired, and mildly mentally retarded . . . and the nursery schools were not even mildly interested in taking these children into their programs," Broida said. "The reason was not because they were insensitive. The reason was because they had no idea how to care for them."

School officials were alarmed at the lack of preschool services for these children. The situation also brought home the importance of educating high school students planning careers in child care on how to deal with handicapped children in a preschool setting.

In an effort to address both problems, the Pinellas County Board of Education opened a child care service for moderately handicapped children at St. Petersburg's Lakewood High School and brought home economics students in to observe the class. Funding came from a preschool incentive grant, the federal grant that was the precursor to the new 3 through 5 program in the 1986 Education of the Handicapped Act Amendments.

But the general student population in the northern section of the district was mushrooming while the preschool population in St. Petersburg, in the south, was shrinking. By 1984, school officials thought it was time to move the program and, at the same time, increase high school students' involvement in it by developing a curriculum that meshed early education services with a high school class on child care.

A grant from the U.S. Education Department's Handicapped Children's Early Education Program helped the district establish such a class at Countryside High School in a Clearwater suburb. A program manager and secretary to develop the curriculum came with the three-year, $258,000 grant. The district provided the special education and home economics teachers and teacher's aide to run the new class. The High School/Preschool Partnership Program was born.

The partnership class at Countryside High School is the only one of the county's four programs for handicapped preschoolers that teams preschool and high school students (two others are self-contained special education preschools and the third is a child care program located at an adult vocational training school). It accommodates 10 handicapped youngsters and 20 of their nonhandicapped peers. Child Find identifies eligible handicapped children, and the district evaluates and places them. The program admits nonhandicapped preschoolers on a first-come, first-served basis—maintaining a balance of boys and girls and of 3- and 4-year-olds (handicapped 5-year-olds are served in kindergarten classes), according to Janelle Johnson-Jenkins, former manager of the partnership program.

The High School/Preschool Partnership Program opened to students in February 1984. Here's how it works:

The program built on the three-day-a-week child care center Countryside had used since 1980 as a lab for its vocational child care students. Under the partnership, handicapped youngsters attend the lab school every day, riding to and from school on the same buses that carry the high school students because the district cannot afford separate transportation. The nonhandicapped preschoolers continue to attend three days a week, and their families pay a $10 registration fee plus $3 a week for tuition. Families of handicapped students pay nothing.

High school students must take a child development course as a prerequisite for the child care lab. About 25 juniors and seniors get into the child care program. Once admitted, they receive five weeks of classroom instruction — team taught by the child care and Varying Exceptionalities teachers — before beginning their 13-week session in the lab school, working under the supervision of the Varying Exceptionalities teacher, the child care teacher and an aide. High school students work in the preschool three days a week for two class periods — approximately two hours — a day.

"It's all orchestrated to the advantage of the child in the program and also to the experience of the high school student taking the home economics courses," said Jonathan McIntire, supervisor for Pinellas County's Low Prevalence Programs.

"It's a wonderful opportunity for high school students to see that even though these children are handicapped and they do need special attention in some special circumstances, they are more normal than abnormal. It really nullifies the stereotypes they may have coming into the class," he said.

"One of the hopes we have for these high school students and one of the beliefs we have is, because these people will become the people working in local day care programs, because they know handicapped children are more normal than abnormal, they will open up more doors for handicapped [children] outside the school system," he added.

But while the program seemed the answer to many of the educators' needs, not all parents were convinced. "We had underestimated some things," said Broida. "A lot of time has to go into public relations and acceptance."

One objection many parents of handicapped children had was to enrolling their children in a program located at a high school and putting them on a high school bus. School officials dealt with the reservations by approaching the parents they thought would be most receptive.

One was a mother who had recently moved from Georgia, where her child received extensive preschool services. In Florida she had found no services and was becoming extremely frustrated. "She was one of the first in the program," said Broida. "That's the type of parents we were involved with at the time. We told them there was the possibility of a program and they were thrilled to death."

Educators met one-on-one with parents of handicapped children, conducted tours of the facility, trained bus drivers and designated teams of high school students to act as "big buddies" to the youngsters while they were on the buses.

Barbara Whatley, whose 3-year-old daughter, Alyssa, was the program's youngest handicapped participant in the 1986-87 school year, said "it was kind of scary to think she'd be going to a high school, and Countryside is the biggest high school in this county. I think my husband was more concerned than I was, but when we visited the program last spring we could see the program was contained by itself away from the high school activity."

Partnership staff also had to work with the families of nonhandicapped youngsters already enrolled in the child care lab, explaining the nature of the program and the handicaps of the other children. "There was some hesitance in the beginning with parents wondering 'What kind of children are my kids going to be with,'" said Wendy Swertfeger, the special education teacher in the partnership program.

But, said McIntire, "After the first spring, we had people breaking down the door to get their [handicapped] kids in."

In three years of operation the partnership seems to have accomplished its goals. Johnson-Jenkins said surveys of parent and student attitudes, as well as studies on the preschoolers' progress, show parents believe their children are being served well, high school students are becoming more interested in special education careers, and handicapped students' socialization skills are enhanced by their contact with their nonhandicapped peers and with high school students.

Kim Teunis, a senior in the program, said that as a result of her experience in the lab, she has shifted her career plans from child care education to special education or child psychology. In the partnership's first year, Teunis noted, few students understood what the course was or even knew the school offered it. That has changed.

"A lot of people are trying to get in, and quite a few get turned down. I think we've spread the word around that it's not just an easy class, that you really go do something," she said.

The word also has moved through the educational community. In 1984 supervisors of Pinellas County's adult vocational education program asked Johnson-Jenkins to write a curriculum guide to launch a similar program at the St. Petersburg Vocational Technical School. That program opened in 1985.

Johnson-Jenkins, who relinquished management of the partnership when its federal grant expired in 1986, said once curriculum and administrative guides are written, a district can easily continue the program on its own at little cost. Schools can enlist the talents of the special education and home economics teachers they already have. The aide's salary and materials for the program would represent the only added cost.

McIntire said he believes the success of a program such as the partnership is determined by "chemistry and commitment, and I would stress commitment. This works if you have people who are flexible and who are willing to work with the model, but it doesn't work if you have people who have built their own world and don't want anyone messing around with it."

Case Study 3.3

Program: Early Childhood Education Program, Urbana, Ill., School District

Summary: Two early childhood education classes serve all children in the district ages 3 through 5 who are eligible for special education services. There is no waiting list and no charge for the program.

Contacts: 1. Donna Crawford, Urbana School District #116, Early Childhood Office, Wiley Administration Center, P.O. Box 3039, 1602 S. Anderson, Urbana, Ill. 61801, (217)384-3616
2. Richard Bodine, principal, Leal Elementary School, 312 W. Oregon, Urbana, Ill. 61801, (217)384-3618
3. Debbie Heater, parent, Rural Route Three, Box No. 127B, Urbana, Ill. 61801, (217)367-6067

Debbie Heater first suspected something was wrong when her infant daughter, Kimberly, struggled futilely to hold up her head. And while most other babies her age were rolling over with ease, Kimberly could not begin to do so.

Keeping a close eye on Kimberly's development for two years, Mrs. Heater took her at the first available opportunity to the Urbana, Ill., School District's Early Childhood Office for a free developmental screening. Specialists in the office diagnosed muscular and speech deficiencies and recommended Kimberly for a state-sponsored preschool program where she would receive occupational and speech therapy.

When she enrolled in the program at age three, Kimberly was testing well behind her peers in language and motor development. By the time she turned 5, however, she was adapting well to kindergarten and testing "right on grade level," her mother said. "She's a little stick of dynamite — short, hefty and ready to go," Mrs. Heater added proudly.

Without the special attention offered by Urbana's free preschool program, Mrs. Heater said, "I shudder to think what would have happened to Kimberly." She probably would have been a "very frustrated and angry child" who would have started kindergarten with handicaps that could have held her back for life.

Kimberly Heater is one of hundreds of children Urbana's early childhood education program has served since the mid-seventies. As early as 1973, when the nation was just beginning to wake up to its responsibilities to children with special needs, Urbana was offering free testing and individualized learning programs with the goal of serving every handicapped child in the district.

Mrs. Heater first learned of the district's Wiley Preschool when her oldest daughter, Terry, was 3. Terry had experienced several ear infections and "wasn't pronouncing things right," according to her mother. Diagnosticians from the school district visited Terry's child care provider, tested the child and determined her eligible for the district's daily special preschool program. Mrs. Heater didn't have to worry about additional expenses or transportation; the district did not charge her for preschool services and provided bus transportation to and from its students' child care centers.

The program made a believer of Mrs. Heater. Terry "couldn't wait for the bus to come" to take her to preschool, she said. "I received constant updates telling me what she was doing and suggesting things I could practice with her at home." By the time Terry was in second grade, she was talking "too much and too clear," her mother joked.

Mrs. Heater was so impressed with the program and Terry's progress at Wiley Preschool that she volunteered to become president of the school's Parent/Teacher Association in 1985. After Kimberly "graduated" in 1986, Mrs. Heater no longer had children in the school but stayed on as head of the PTA because of her commitment to the early childhood education program. "It's a remarkable program," she said.

From its beginning in 1973, Urbana's early childhood education program has attempted to meet special needs of children in the least restrictive environment with a strong emphasis on involving and educating parents. "We have a real wide range in terms of abilities and backgrounds," said Donna Crawford, program director. While teachers try not to categorize the abilities of children at such a young age, the school does limit attendance to children deemed trainable and educable. Nearly all of the students end up going to a regular kindergarten when they reach age 5.

The Urbana preschool program, which is housed in a former elementary school, serves an average of 120 children each year through a combination of federal, state and local funding. Crawford expected the 1986 Education of the Handicapped Act Amendments, P.L. 99-457, to bring in more money for the program by fiscal year 1988. That, she hoped, would allow the school to expand from two and a half hours a day, which "never seems to be enough time" to provide occupational and speech and language therapy.

Increased enrollment in higher grades and the need for a full-day kindergarten program, however, have placed the preschool program in a delicate political situation. The district projected a need for 27 more elementary school classrooms between 1987 and 1992. Taking this increase into account, the district also projected a drop in preschool enrollment, from an average of 125 to 90, and a reduction in the number of preschool teachers and classes from the 1987 level of 11.

Expecting such reductions in preschool enrollment was unrealistic, both Heater and Crawford maintained. "It should be an expanding program," Heater said. "There are still parents who don't know about it and children who are not being served." Since the Urbana preschool program is located in a former elementary school and since it shares space with district administrative offices, it is a prime candidate for space reduction, Heater said. Parents and teachers would have to be forceful advocates to be sure the program received a fair shake, she added.

Because the early childhood education program is a full-fledged part of the Urbana School District, teachers at Wiley Preschool work closely with elementary school teachers to ease students' transition from preschool to public school. Both groups "very definitely consider each other colleagues," Crawford said. It "took a few years to develop," she said, but a strong relationship has been well-established since the mid-1970s.

Richard Bodine, principal of Leal Elementary School, where many of the preschoolers transfer, said an excellent transitional liaison exists between his school and the preschool program. Kindergarten teachers consult regularly with preschool teachers. Elementary school specialists check out the preschool children in the spring before they begin kindergarten and receive the children's records well before the new school year begins.

Children who have attended the preschool program "do very well the first semester" in kindergarten, Bodine said. "They are well attuned to the whole process of learning. They know their strengths and how to use them. They know the rules of how to get along with one another."

After the first semester, the advantages most children obtained in the preschool program tend to level out, Bodine said. This generally is true of Head Start-type programs, he added.

Urbana's Wiley Preschool conducts two early childhood education sections for children ages 3 to 5. Children with special needs attend school from 8:30 a.m. to 11:30 a.m., and low-income children who need school readiness experience attend from noon to 2:30 p.m.

Children enrolled in the first section receive special education in one or more areas of development. The classes are limited to 11 children taught by a certified early childhood special education teacher with the assistance of a teacher's aide.

Children attending the second section do not receive special education services but do receive speech and language therapy. Up to 20 children attend afternoon classes, taught by an early childhood education teacher and a teacher's aide.

The program surveys parents at the beginning and end of each school year, and, Crawford said, "We receive very few complaints." The largest number of complaints involved transportation logistics.

The program educates parents as well. Teachers try to arrange conferences several times during the year, including home visits. The school puts out a newsletter for parents, offers day and evening workshops on parenting special needs children and encourages parents to drop in to visit the school. (On Mondays, parents can drop in without an appointment to observe their children in class and to ask questions.) The school also provides a list of eight possibilities for parent involvement, ranging from volunteering as teacher's aides to working on the school newsletter.

"The parents in the program are as individual and special as the children themselves," states a written description of the program's learning philosophy provided to each parent. "Therefore, the approach taken with each family member needs to be as individualized as the classroom instruction for their child. The parents will have a wide variety of services and activities available as they become involved in the early developmental education of their children. Each parent is capable of growth — the amount of growth of individual parents will vary. The extent to which a parent progresses is dependent upon the degree to which he or she becomes involved."

Not only does the program strive to increase parental knowledge about their child's development, it also suggests specific ways to cope with stress encountered in parenting, provides parents with a list of their child's rights and responsibilities, and explains how child-teacher relationships are developed.

Crawford said the Urbana program benefits from its location in the same community as the University of Illinois. She works closely with the university's early childhood education department. The university influence also adds a diversity to the preschool population, creating a situation in which children from different backgrounds help each other learn. "We have parents who are university professors and parents who are lower income," Crawford said.

The biggest shortcoming of the program, Crawford said, is the limited number of hours each day that children attend the school. And while the program works with child care centers and provides bus transportation to and from the centers, it does not provide child care itself. Crawford said the program is also in need of more space and more support staff.

The program has no waiting list. It has a mandate from the state to screen and serve all the preschool children in the community who have special needs. And the state backs up the mandate with commensurate pay for teachers. While private preschool teachers across the nation are notoriously underpaid—far below the scale even for public school teachers—preschool teachers of special needs students in Illinois receive salaries equal to those of other public school teachers. Most of the 11 teachers in the Urbana program have a masters degree with five or six years experience. In 1986, they earned an average of about $21,000.

"We're very proud of our program," Crawford said, "even though we realize there's always more to be done."

Chapter Four

Personnel Preparation: Meeting The Demand

States today face a critical shortage of personnel qualified to serve the youngest handicapped children, and the demands of P.L. 99-457 can only aggravate the problem. State policymakers face the challenge of coping with personnel gaps in the present while cultivating a new generation of qualified staff for the future.

Nearly 90 percent of states in 1986 reported they lacked sufficient personnel to adequately serve their handicapped children from birth through age 2, while 80 percent said they could not provide full services to children ages 3 through 5, according to a study by the universities of Michigan and North Carolina. Most states expect the problem to continue at least until 1989.

Even states that mandated services for handicapped preschoolers before the 1986 Education of the Handicapped Act Amendments are struggling. To compensate for the lack of qualified personnel, they're using the "band-aid approach to dealing with shortages," said Judy Smith-Davis, a noted authority on training personnel to educate the handicapped and coauthor of the book *Personnel to Educate the Handicapped in America: A Status Report* (Institute for the Study of Exceptional Children and Youth, 1986).

Many states are issuing emergency or temporary teaching certificates to fill the void in school-based programs, placing teachers with no preschool special education training in early childhood classrooms and giving them a period of grace in which to earn an appropriate certificate, said Smith-Davis, who also is editor of the quarterly special education publication, *Counterpoint*. In other states, rural districts are grouping children with varying disabilities and needs in one classroom to conserve personnel.

Universities could alleviate teacher shortages by creating more early childhood special education programs, but most institutions face budget problems and are reluctant to start programs in states where the personnel demand is weak. Most states allow generally certified teachers to conduct early childhood special education programs, thus discouraging universities from offering specialized early childhood training.

Unless states mandate programs to train early childhood special education personnel, "universities won't meet the demand," predicted John Melcher, an early childhood consultant with the Frank Porter Graham Child Development Center in Chapel Hill and

Wisconsin's special education director from 1956 to 1975.

An even worse problem exists with infant intervention programs. There is a dearth of infant services training programs in the country — far fewer than training programs that focus on 3 to 5 year olds — because of the rarity of mandates for the youngest children.

Only seven states mandate services for handicapped children from birth, another 19 require them from ages 2, 3 or 4, and the rest mandate them from ages 5 or 6, according to the U.S. Education Department (see Appendix B). For states planning to expand their mandates for handicapped children, building a pool of qualified personnel will be a piecemeal process.

If states that already have gone through the process are any indication, they will spend several years in transition — setting standards, outlining university curricula, issuing emergency teaching certificates and providing inservice training. States will have to rely on stopgap measures while they wait for a new generation of service providers to complete four to five years of early childhood training.

It's a slow process, but it works. States like Nebraska and Iowa that mandated services to infants and toddlers in the mid-1970s found themselves a decade later issuing fewer emergency certificates and placing more teachers with appropriate preservice training in early childhood special education classes.

How Four States Deal With Shortages

Tennessee The special education teacher shortage in Tennessee only gets worse. Although the state mandates services for handicapped children beginning at age 4, it requires no special certificate for early childhood special educators. Jane Williams, director of state certification for Tennessee's education department, says a specialized certificate requirement would encourage more universities to provide early childhood training. This would, in turn, increase the teacher supply in that field.

"Institutions follow the requirements of a state. It's pretty difficult for colleges to provide programs if [the state] doesn't offer a certificate," said Williams. Just two or three of Tennessee's 38 training institutions offer programs in early childhood special education, she added.

Although Tennessee has waived its special education certification requirements, it still has not been able to fill 44 vacancies in special education classrooms around the state, Williams said. Under the waiver, teachers with general certificates — usually elementary school teachers — can teach handicapped children but must prove they can earn a special education certificate in two years.

South Carolina "Our shortage is so great that there's hardly any way to measure it," said Helen Geesey, state planning coordinator for South Carolina's education department.

The University of South Carolina, the only school in the state with an early childhood special education program, graduates only five or six teachers a year in that field, Geesey said.

Anticipating the amendments to the Education of the Handicapped Act, the state in June 1986 began to collaborate with other universities in the state to develop early childhood special education standards and has approached universities and training institutions to create early childhood programs.

A major part of the state's training plan is teaching psychologists to assess the needs of handicapped preschoolers, Geesey explained. The University of South Carolina in Columbia already offers this training.

To staff preschool programs in the meantime, the state plans to hire teachers who have either early childhood or special education degrees and offer them inservice training, said Geesey. "Hopefully within the next three to five years we'll have a pool of people who have gone through the right type of training."

Nebraska The early childhood personnel shortage has lessened in Nebraska, one of seven states that offers services to handicapped children from birth. The state set the mandate in the 1979-1980 school year and by 1987 was ready to eliminate the waiver system it had used to fill personnel gaps, said Jan Thelen, grants coordinator for the early childhood special education division of the Nebraska Department of Education.

"Now our training programs are well established. Early childhood special education is a field unto itself," said Thelen. To be fully qualified to teach early childhood special education in Nebraska, teachers must have specialized training, she said.

Thelen said the first few years of building early childhood training programs are "pretty rough." In 1979 none of Nebraska's state universities offered a specialized program, and the first few early childhood programs that started "looked good on paper but were poor in quality." It wasn't until August 1980 that Nebraska developed standards for university early childhood special education programs, Thelen added.

To staff preschool services before university training programs emerged, the state called on a valuable pool of highly trained specialists in early childhood disabilities, professionals serving handicapped children through the state office of mental retardation. School districts hired these specialists "because we didn't want to lose that expertise at the time we needed it most," Thelen explained.

After the state devised an early childhood special education certificate, it "grandfathered" these professionals into the schools without requiring them to earn teaching credentials.

Nebraska also hired teachers with either an early childhood or special education certificate and offered inservice training to develop the skills the teachers lacked. The state tried to avoid hiring teachers with only elementary school certificates, said Thelen.

When it expanded its special education mandate, Nebraska intensified its inservice training. Under an arrangement between the state education department and two training institutions, teachers can take courses specific to their needs on weekday evenings and weekends without having to travel to the training campus. Trainers come to schools or other convenient locations.

Iowa Since 1975 Iowa has served handicapped children from birth. The state still suffers shortages of early childhood special educators, but has developed a training system worth noting.

Iowa phased in training requirements gradually before it added a new early childhood qualification requirement to its special education certificate, said Joan Turner Clary, an early childhood special education consultant to the Iowa Education Department.

Prior to the new requirement, special education teachers had to complete eight credit hours in early childhood education to earn a temporary certificate. When the state decided to require more early childhood coursework, teachers who already had completed eight hours received permanent certification, Clary said.

"It has to be piecemeal for a while. You have to take what you have and then build from that," she said.

To devise its new certification plan, the education department asked for recommendations from local training institutions, teachers, administrators and Chapter 1 preschool program directors. Clary said Iowa also researched other states' early childhood special education programs.

The state then put its money into inservice training. Consultants experienced in working with severely handicapped individuals conducted training sessions of up to three weeks for teachers, and early childhood experts came in from other states to run workshops.

Iowa still hires teachers with temporary certificates and gives them two years to complete the full certificate. Recognizing the cramped schedules of full-time teachers, the state initiated a new inservice training program that allows temporarily certified personnel to meet course requirements without having to travel to a university campus, said Kathleen McCarton, assistant professor of child development at Iowa State University.

The program, which operates on a U.S. Education Department

personnel preparation grant, provides lectures on videotape. Clary said Iowa also has used a statewide computer network to conduct inservice training at 15 to 17 sites simultaneously, which has been "real effective" for teaching about genetics, spinal defects and stimulation of premature infants.

The state may expand inservice training to provide student teacher experiences for temporarily certified personnel, McCarton said. Teachers would take a one-month leave of absence from their regular job to teach and be supervised in an early childhood special education class, she said.

Clary emphasized that it takes time for a new delivery system to go into full swing. Hospitals and other medical facilities that diagnose and refer handicapped children must realize a new program is available for the youngsters, she said.

Now that federal preschool incentive grant funds have reduced the state's contribution to inservice training, Clary said, Iowa can give more attention to developing infant intervention services. "The population has changed through the years. We're finding kids at a much younger age than we originally did," said Clary. "Those kids are usually really handicapped, and teachers find themselves working with a much more medically fragile population."

The Fine Line Of Certification

Developing personnel standards is essential to building a strong corps of qualified early childhood special education professionals.

But in devising these standards, states are faced with a difficult policy challenge. The standards must be tough enough to ensure preparedness, yet reasonable enough so people from various service delivery systems can meet them.

Seventeen states are ensuring classroom readiness by requiring teachers to earn preschool special education teaching certificates or by adding early childhood education requirements to general special education certificates, according to *Personnel to Educate the Handicapped In America*.

But specialized certification has its drawbacks and is not the only avenue to personnel preparation.

Specialized certification requirements prolong a state's teacher shortage. States that require only general special education certification can pull from a large pool of special educators to fill their preschool programs. But it takes time to train teachers for an early childhood special education career, especially if a state decides to require a master's degree for certification.

School administrators also would have less flexibility to transfer specialized teachers to fill personnel needs in other grades or academic areas.

The need for a specialized certificate, or even any teaching certificate, might also discourage professionals in the developmental disabilities field from working in school-based programs. Experts question the need for a trained developmental disabilities professional to complete core teaching courses before stepping into the classroom.

Specialized certification also may get in the way of integrating handicapped and nonhandicapped children. If states require preschool special education teachers to have a specialized certificate, "then they won't be able to put kids in Head Start and nursery school," where teachers must meet different standards, said Gloria Harbin, associate director of state policies for the State Technical Assistance Resource Team (START) program at the Frank Porter Graham Center.

For example, the California Department of Education will not subsidize a handicapped child served in a program in which no staff member has a general special education certificate.

States that developed early mandates to serve handicapped preschoolers are doing a poor job of integrating those children with their nonhandicapped peers, said Harbin. "Least restrictive environment is pretty much nonexistent at the preschool level." Head Start, even though it does not require its teachers to have education degrees, is one of the best models for serving handicapped children together with nonhandicapped students, she said.

* * *

CEC Guidelines As states brood individually over personnel standards, the Council for Exceptional Children (CEC) is developing model special education training criteria, as well as deciding what areas of specialization are needed, said Frederick Weintraub, assistant executive director. CEC is trying to determine whether special requirements or certificates should be developed according to areas of disability or age.

"Right now, there's no rhyme or reason out there in the field as to who ought to be qualified" to work with handicapped preschoolers. CEC, which also serves as the special education arm of the National Council for the Accreditation of Teacher Education, expects to release certification standards in spring 1987. Universities would have to comply with the standards before their programs could be accredited.

CEC will determine the need for an early preschool special education certificate, as well as the need for a certificate with special focus on serving the birth through 2 population, Weintraub said.

"Ideally, what states would like is a special educator who is also certified in elementary and secondary. . . . You can just move that person around. However, that doesn't serve the interests of the child," he said.

"You shouldn't [develop] standards because you need lots of warm bodies. On the other hand, you can't have standards that put you in a position where you can't run programs."

Weintraub and Harbin both support a compromise plan in which teachers with general education backgrounds would be supervised by trained or specially certified early childhood special education teachers. This approach would facilitate integration of handicapped and nonhandicapped children, said Harbin.

* * *

In California, a team of professionals developing personnel standards for the state's preschool special education teachers are considering a similar model. The team hopes to establish a generic set of competencies "that all agencies will buy into," according to Linda Brekken, coordinator of the state education department's infant preschool special education research network.

Requiring a teaching certificate would alienate qualified professionals from other fields, such as occupational and physical therapists and psychologists, who would have to go back to school to earn general teaching credentials, Brekken said.

Instead, the standards should allow for the use of personnel without formal education training, she added. Urban areas such as Watts or East Los Angeles need people who know the language, culture and community of the children they serve.

Personnel without formal training also would be helpful in infant service programs, where staff work very closely with families of handicapped babies. They could work under an infant services specialist while receiving inservice training to improve their skills, said Brekken.

* * *

Massachusetts is considering merging two certificates — early childhood education and early childhood special education — to facilitate integration at the preschool level.

The state has had an early childhood special education certificate since about 1979, said Carole Thomson, director of Massachusetts' Chapter 188 program, which in 1985 established a state-funded preschool program for disadvantaged children. In 1987 the state started developing early childhood education certification requirements for the Chapter 188 program.

The joint certificate would solve the certification obstacle to integrating handicapped and disadvantaged preschoolers, according to Thomson. Chapter 188 teachers would be qualified to teach any handicapped preschooler placed in their classrooms.

The proposal is prompting a great deal of discussion around the state, said Thomson. Because the undergraduate joint certificate could be completed in the same amount of time as a single specialty certificate, colleges and universities question whether they will have time to adequately prepare teachers in both areas, she said.

Other universities "think it's not an issue," Thomson said. They suggest that regular education and special education faculty share the training task.

Serving Infants

Infant intervention is a new and foreign field for education policymakers, although states have in the past served handicapped infants through fragmented delivery systems that rely on professionals in the physical and occupational therapy, developmental disabilities and medical communities.

Since 1985 the U.S. Education Department's Office of Special Education Programs has awarded grants to support infant training programs and help fill personnel gaps. Incentive for states to train infant service specialists is even greater under P.L. 99-457.

The law requires states to have organized personnel development plans if they seek federal assistance for the fifth operating year of infant services programs. "This component is one of the most important in the system. Without qualified personnel," the successes envisioned by the program will not occur, the House Education and Labor Committee wrote in its report on the bill that became the 1986 Education of the Handicapped Act Amendments.

Before P.L. 99-457, various state agencies serving handicapped infants had developed their own personnel requirements, resulting in a hodge-podge of staff criteria ranging from a high school diploma to a doctorate in infant care.

But even degree-granting birth to 5 personnel training programs are criticized for false advertising. Many of these programs focus on

Personnel Preparation

preschool and lack the curriculum and expertise to prepare personnel to work with infants.

Very few university birth to 5 programs stress infant intervention competencies, said Diane Bricker, professor of special education at the University of Oregon and an evaluator of infant programs nationwide. "It's very scary that they're turning out people who work with [infants] that don't know what they're doing."

States must devise training criteria for infant service personnel that develop skills different from those needed to serve handicapped preschoolers. To do this, they can look to the few model infant service training programs in the country that offer a multidisciplinary or transdisciplinary approach to learning. These programs blend the expertise of the medical, education and social welfare communities to provide a wholistic approach to serving handicapped infants.

Two competencies are essential to infant intervention—medical knowledge and family assistance skills. Infant service personnel should be able to evaluate infants with overt physical disabilities very early. They also must be able to work not only with the baby, but also with a family still shocked at the arrival of a handicapped child.

* * *

George Washington University One program that does focus on infant intervention can be found at Wheelock College in Boston (see Case Study 4.1). Another is the Infant Special Education program at George Washington University in Washington, D.C. The program, which offers both a master's and post-master's degree in infant intervention, accepts students from a variety of backgounds and prepares them to care for children from birth through age 2 using a multidisciplinary team approach. The team is a diverse group of professionals that provides medical, instructional and case management services for handicapped children and their families.

Most people who enter the program "are already in the field and are intrigued by the complexity of the special ed kids they're asked to treat," said program coordinator Maxine Freund. "The program broadens their focus."

Professionals from fields such as physical and occupational therapy and special education exit the master's degree program as infant specialists. The program's goal is to give the student an understanding of the unique roles the different professions play in serving a handicapped infant.

Teamwork is the key to successful infant intervention, and students at George Washington University learn to synthesize and coordinate services from the various fields into a "comprehensive educational program," according to the program's written description. This approach qualifies such professionals as physical and occupational therapists to work as special educators after graduation, Freund said.

To be eligible for the master's degree program, students must have a bachelor's degree from an accredited college or university and professional experience in a field related to infant intervention. "Most of our master's students have been out in the field three to five to seven years," Freund said. "They're real savvy people. We're very cautious about taking a neophyte."

Designed to meet the needs of working special education professionals, the master's Infant Special Education program is a part-time, 39 semester-hour program that can be completed in two years.

Master's degree candidates examine how specific handicapping conditions affect infant development and study the developmental stages of parenting, with special emphasis on how families can better cope with raising a handicapped child and the variety of community services available to assist parents with handicapped infants.

"When you're treating an at-risk infant, you're not just treating the infant. You're treating a grieving, disappointed family," said Freund.

Coursework for both programs includes study of infant motor development, providing special education professionals with a wider knowledge base to help them work with health-related professionals; the structure, function of, and access to, service agencies most needed by handicapped children and their families; various approaches used by interagency service programs; strategies for assessing the handicaps and needs of high-risk infants; and the impact of certain treatments of genetically-linked handicapping conditions.

Internships and practical experience are essential parts of the program. Students, while pursuing their degree, must work in an infant intervention program for at least 420 hours.

Master's degree interns assess infants and design education objectives they then help the infants work toward. They also suggest appropriate referrals for the infants, work with related personnel and participate in parent conferences.

Graduates of the post-master's degree program, which requires 30 additional credit hours, are qualified to design and administer their own infant intervention programs, either in the private or public sector. As in the master's degree program, the post-master's degree program is geared toward integrating medical and education training.

Applicants for the post-master's degree program must have either a master of arts or master of sciences degree in education or a related field and two years experience in a field related to infant intervention.

The coursework takes an administrative approach to intervention, offering studies in developing home, school and community support systems for handicapped infants and their families; planning, implementing, monitoring and evaluating early intervention programs; administering and supervising special education programs; consultation skills; legal issues; and public policy relating to social services.

For the post-master's training program, George Washington University prefers students remain employed in their respective fields to "lend richness to the training," according to the program description. Students take courses in the evening or during vacations, and the program makes individual arrangements for experience in the field. Internships for post-master's degree candidates involve college teaching, program administration, personnel supervision or working with private agencies.

* * *

With new federal funds available to help develop personnel training programs in infant services, federal grant officials expect a surge of grant proposals, but worry about their quality.

Universities may "slap together a program just to get the money," said Sandy Hazen, personnel preparation project officer for the U.S. Education Department's Office of Special Education Programs. A fifth to a third of these grant writers will be "people who don't have much of a sense of the area they're applying for. I don't know what we'd be reaching down to," she said.

With the funding competition for infant training grants heating up, "people want to get in and get their share of the money. It's understandable but worrisome," said the Univerity of Oregon's Bricker.

Proposals will come from universities that "have no knowledge of [infant] programs" because it's happening so quickly, said START's Harbin.

Bricker offered the following advice. Institutions interested in developing personnel training programs in infant services should research and visit model programs in other states. They also should consult with professionals who have established programs.

Bricker also warned institutions, because of the medical needs involved in preparing personnel to work with handicapped infants, not to pursue infant intervention training if they don't have access to a medical facility or lack experienced faculty members. Institutions in rural areas may be less equipped to start infant intervention training programs, she added.

University politics also may play a part in the search for professionals to head new university infant programs, Harbin said. The best qualified candidate may not end up getting the job. Universities often value candidates who have published their research over those who haven't published, but who have started infant training programs, she said.

* * *

As states try to develop high-level infant training programs, communities continue to serve handicapped infants with smaller innovative programs that sidestep institutionalization.

The Family Support and Resource Center in Madison, Wis., started a family support program in 1983 with the help of a demonstration grant from the Wisconsin Council on Developmental Disabilities. By 1987 its operating budget was $300,000 and was entirely subsidized by the state and the county, according to Linda Brown, president of the center's board of directors in 1986.

The program serves families of all incomes on a sliding fee scale and charges no family more than $3,000 a year. The program provides a variety of services to help ease the stress of caring for a handicapped child.

"We go into the home and say, 'What would make your life easier?' like helping to pay for diapers or maybe a piece of equipment the child needs for physical therapy," said Brown.

Many families turn to the support program after other social service agencies have turned them away. One rural family asked for help to build a barrier around their wood stove so their retarded child would not burn herself when they weren't watching. And Brown herself, who has a multiply handicapped son, could not get state funds to buy the cordless phone she needed for the times she had to call a rescue squad while administering cardio-pulmonary resuscitation to her son. The family support program helps fill the gaps in such situations.

The program also provides a babysitting service for parents who want to get away for a night or a weekend, but can't find anyone to care for their handicapped infant.

The program has a staff of seven, three part-time and four full-time employees. Staff in both programs have backgrounds in special education, social work or both. Personnel must have a degree in human services or social work or have experience working with families of disabled persons.

When it opened in 1983, the family support program launched an intensive outreach campaign, soliciting referrals from doctors, hospitals and agencies that serve children. By 1987 the program had a waiting list of 60 families.

"This is the first year we didn't solicit to get people — we're at the limit," Brown said.

Serving Rural Areas

States continue to suffer the greatest personnel shortages in rural areas, a problem that is independent of resource and funding issues. Many people simply don't want to live in underdeveloped, sometimes desolate areas. And lack of transportation and access to other medical facilities only makes the service problem worse.

Experts have suggested a few recruitment techniques, but it is unclear to what extent they are being used.

In Pennsylvania, a largely rural state, some training institutions send students to rural areas to fulfill their student teaching requirements. The hope is that they will remain after their practicum is over, according to Gary Makuch, state special education director.

But although the governor has decided to accept federal funds for birth through 2 programs, Makuch said, "right now we have no particular plan" to service rural areas.

Another alternative is to locate people already living in rural areas who are interested in special education. These people can attend training institutions around the state, then return to their communities.

One problem special education teachers in rural areas face is the lack of a peer group. In most cases, they are the only such specialist in the community, said David Stockford, Maine's state director of special education. These teachers need a support system, "which is problematic when they're spread over [large] areas," he said.

Human desires also add to rural shortages. "Most personnel working with infants are unmarried young women who don't want to be stuck out in Timbuktu" where their social lives might atrophy, said the University of Oregon's Bricker.

Higher salaries are one obvious means of drawing personnel to underpopulated areas. But that isn't an option for many rural states, which also are suffering economically.

Using Allied Health Professionals

Allied health professionals — a group that includes occupational and physical therapists and speech, language and hearing pathologists — are a major source of services for handicapped children and, like other trained service providers, are in short supply.

Allied health representatives exercised a strong hand in shaping P.L. 99-457, making sure the law recognized their importance and encouraged programs to hire well-trained allied health professionals. They also were responsible for changing the law's categorization of occupational and physical therapy and several other health-related services from a related to a primary service for infants and toddlers.

This change will allow infants and toddlers in need of neurological therapy to receive it without having to show a need for special education. Before P.L. 99-457 handicapped children evaluated for special education services had to show a need for special instruction — for handicapped infants and toddlers, learning such concepts as size and quantity — before they could qualify for "related" physical and occupational therapy services.

Policymakers changed the categorization because they realized neurological stimulation may be more appropriate for infants than special instruction, said Gray Garwood, who was staff director for the House Select Education Subcommittee during the development of P.L. 99-457.

Children diagnosed as having been handicapped from infancy probably have physical and motor problems. Many times these infants must be taught to roll over, sit up and eat, services an occupational therapists provides, said Barbara Hanft, assistant director of government and legal affairs for the American Occupational Therapy Association.

But because the new law accentuates allied health services, experts expect an increase in birth through 2 programs will aggravate an already acute shortage of qualified professionals.

In January 1986, 29 states already faced a shortage of physical therapists, with five reporting severe problems, according to *Personnel To Educate the Handicapped In America*. The study also showed 28 states suffered from a shortage of occupational therapists, with five of them in severe trouble.

"There's going to be a real strong manpower shortage," said Hanft. "I don't see the field opening up that much because we can't train any more therapists than we do now — unless there's more money."

State and private universities do the training with a mix of federal and state funding, although most of the funding comes from the states, said Hanft.

Personnel Preparation

And while some programs may not be able to locate the occupational therapists they need, others would rather not hire professionals who aren't "education personnel." For example, some schools fill the void by asking gym teachers to provide the service, said Hanft. "Part of the problem is they don't understand how therapists can help teachers in the classroom."

Her association recommends three models of assistance occupational therapists (OTs) can provide a classroom teacher. Under the first model, the OT is a one-time consultant to the teacher, suggesting activities and methods of working with handicapped children. Under the second approach, OTs can take a more active role as classroom monitors, evaluating a student's needs and recommending an appropriate individualized education program (IEP) for the child. OTs under this model would not actually work with the child.

If a child's nervous system is very fragile, the association recommends a third model in which an OT can directly treat the student. "If a child is fragile, [he or she] may be likely to asphyxiate during a meal. Maybe a regular teacher won't pick up on the warning signs," said Hanft.

Schools deal with occupational therapists in a variety of ways. Some contract for their services, some take them on as employees and others contract for services through hospitals. But, said Hanft, "When you get to that point, you don't have a good medical-educational merge." Hospitals look at a child more from a medical-neurological standpoint.

Hanft said she plans to solicit U.S. Education Department funds to help train OTs to work in early intervention programs. Under a grant proposal she is writing, OTs would receive inservice training in pediatrics and family interaction.

"Family interaction and how you relate to family needs is paramount during the first few years" of a handicapped child's life, Hanft said. "Professionals must be skilled to be sensitive to the family's needs and not overload them with things to do."

P.L. 99-457 also encourages states to hire speech and language pathologists with master's degrees. Institutions tend to hire pathologists with bachelor's degrees, while Medicare, Medicaid and other public agencies recognize a master's degree as a minimum level of expertise and training for a pathologist, according to Roger Kingsley, director of congressional relations for the American Speech-Language-Hearing Association.

About 37 states require speech and language pathologists to earn a master's degree before they can work in the private sector or provide services eligible for Medicaid or Medicare reimbursement.

But 19 states don't require public employees to earn a master's degree in speech or language pathology, said Kingsley.

"There's a double standard," he said. "We have studies that show at the bachelor's level people don't have the training to provide services in language development and voice disorders. People at the bachelor's level recognize it themselves."

Why do institutions hire pathologists with only a bachelor's degree? Less qualified teachers typically earn lower salaries, said Kingsley. In other cases, pathologists with only a bachelor's degree may be more plentiful.

"The solution is to provide additional funding to train people at the master's level," said Kingsley. Money should come from either the states or the federal government, he added.

P.L. 99-457 doesn't require programs to follow the same high standards in hiring pathologists as private sector health facilities follow. "This is a state issue and not a federal issue," said congressional aide Gray Garwood. "The feds can't tell the states how to develop state certification."

The new law, however, does require states to outline in their written plans the steps they will take to hire personnel with the same level of training as speech and hearing pathologists in the private sector.

* * *

States must train the personnel to meet the new challenge of providing handicapped services for the youngest children. Finding the people, training them and funding their preparation will require thoughtful, organized plans of action.

With all factions vying for limited personnel preparation grant funds, the key words are caution and coordination. Policymakers must be wary of funding new programs that are ill-structured and poorly staffed. States and training institutions must establish personnel standards that ensure quality while inviting the expertise of professionals outside the education community. And inservice training must be a major concern of programs that hire unqualified or moderately qualified personnel to fill the gaps while they wait for a new generation of early childhood specialists to complete more formal training programs.

From Our Rolodex

Diane Bricker
Center on Human Development
University of Oregon
901 E. 18th St.
Eugene, Ore. 97403
(503)686-3568

Family Support and Resource Center
521 N. Sherman Ave.
Madison, Wis. 53704
(608)246-0414

Roger Kingsley
Director of Congressional Relations
American Speech-Language-Hearing Association
10801 Rockville Pike
Rockville, Md. 20852
(301)897-5700

Jan Thelen
Grants Coordinator
Early Childhood Special Education Division
Nebraska Department of Education
P.O. Box 94987
Lincoln, Neb. 68509
(402)471-2471

Case Study 4.1

Program: Early Intervention: Infants and Toddlers with Special Needs, Wheelock College Graduate School, Boston

Summary: The interdisciplinary program trains graduate students for careers in early intervention with handicapped and at-risk infants and toddlers. Students come from a variety of backgrounds, including education, nursing, social work, speech therapy and occupational therapy.

Contacts: **1.** Susan L. McBride, coordinator, Early Intervention Program, Wheelock College Graduate School, 200 The Riverway, Boston, Mass. 02215, (617)734-5200, ext. 199
2. Lisa Greene, 28 Salem St., Apt. 5, Reading, Mass. 01867, (617)942-1438, or c/o Wheelock College Graduate School

Wheelock College's students don't stay in one place for long. They're expected to understand what happens in the classroom, the hospital and the family unit, because such an interdisciplinary approach is what Wheelock's graduate Early Intervention Program is all about.

The college's infant intervention training program, created in 1981 with a U.S. Education Department personnel preparation grant, is considered one of the best interdisciplinary models in the country because it sends students into the field and expects them to learn to work with families of handicapped babies.

"Almost all [handicapped] children have to spend a lot of time with medical people. So persons in the early intervention field need to understand how the the medical aspects of handicaps impact on the child's needs," said Susan L. McBride, coordinator of Wheelock's early intervention training program. "They must learn how to communicate with medical personnel and, in the end, develop a program that is supportive of the family across settings," including hospitals and the home.

For that reason, courses on the medical aspects of disabling conditions are part of the four-semester master's degree program, which also includes such areas of study as normal infant-toddler development, biological and environmental infant risk factors and infant assessment, according to McBride. Students also learn how to plan a curriculum as part of the program, known as Early Intervention: Infants and Toddlers with Special Needs.

Students in the program work in early intervention programs in the Boston area, including hospitals, under the supervision of both university and on-site program staff, said McBride.

By working in hospitals, the students—even if they don't plan hospital careers—can learn about premature infants and the kinds of special support their families need to make the transition from the neonatal intensive care unit to the home, McBride said.

Another important aspect of the program is its emphasis on the family, said McBride. In 1987 Wheelock planned to request more federal funds to increase the number of supervisors for students working with families. Wheelock also planned to hire a parent of a handicapped child to help teach students about the special needs of handicapped children's families, she added.

That emphasis on the family was a key reason student Lisa Greene, a former special education teacher, chose Wheelock's program. "As a practicing professional, my deficit was that I didn't have a lot of experience with parents," she said. Greene "wanted to switch" from school-age children to infants and toddlers "because I knew a lot of the problems I saw with older children could have or should have been addressed earlier."

Frustration, Greene said, "would be a very good word" for the way she felt in the classroom. "I had several children who were what would be called environmentally at risk, kids whose parents weren't real involved with them, whose parents were into drugs or alcohol, who were raised by single parents on welfare," she said. "Had these kids been picked up a lot earlier, say at birth, and given a lot more experiences, they might have done better in school. By sitting at home until age 5, they weren't really getting a lot of exposure to anything besides alcohol or drugs."

In addition, Greene said, "early intervention might have helped with parent-child interaction, there might have been more constructive interaction. To teach the parents that discipline didn't mean just smacking them around."

Those concerns led Greene to Wheelock, where she can learn how to work with parents both of environmentally at-risk children and of physically or mentally handicapped youngsters. She noted, "There is a lot of frustration in parenting a child like that. Even with a well-behaved, mildly retarded child, parents aren't going to get the same kind of reactions" they would from a nonhandicapped child.

Greene also praised Wheelock's medical curriculum, although she plans a career in an early intervention center, not a hospital, when she graduates in May 1987. Working with premature babies was "extremely helpful," particularly considering her interest in at-risk children. "Seeing them as infants really gave me a greater appreciation for how far they've come by the time I see them in the classroom."

Greene's experience illustrates Wheelock's emphasis on giving its students a better understanding of the services other professionals offer handicapped infants. For instance, McBride said, individuals with backgrounds in nursing, occupational therapy and physical therapy learn how to assess a family's needs and make the proper referrals, while social workers and others with nonmedical backgrounds learn how infants are limited by their physical disabilities.

When students complete Wheelock's program they enter different fields, depending on their previous areas of expertise. Some students with general education backgrounds, for example, have gone on to work in hospital neonatal care units as family liaisons, McBride said.

The placement of Wheelock graduates shows the need for properly trained infant service personnel across the country. Of the 10 students who graduated from the program in fall 1986, only two stayed in Massachusetts to pursue their careers, McBride said.

Another benefit of the infant program, McBride noted, is its close working relationship with Wheelock's other personnel preparation programs, particularly those for preschool and hospital workers. The 40-credit master's preschool program, Teaching Young Children With Special Needs, includes a year-long student teaching practicum, training in individual curriculum planning and interactions with parents and professionals in allied disciplines.

The master's program for those interested in medical settings, Child Life in Hospitals, trains child development specialists who work with infants through adolescents in hospitals and other health care settings. The specialists aim to help families maintain normal living patterns and to minimize the psychological trauma of hospitalization. They plan activities to help children gain a sense of mastery through play, self expression, peer interaction and family involvement.

Through this integrated program, Wheelock believes its students will be able to meet the needs of "the population of children who are being saved by advances in medical technology," according to an abstract of the program. "A group of these children will have chronic medical conditions and, in some cases, severe and multiple handicaps. These children will require special educational services if they are to reach their full potential."

Wheelock's training programs, said the abstract, will produce "a new cadre of early childhood professionals . . . who are highly competent in their own fields of study and prepared to collaborate with each other to service young handicapped children and their families."

Chapter Five

Child Care: The Family's Dilemma

The need for programs that accommodate the schedules of working parents must not be ignored as states devise services for handicapped children from birth through age 5. Child care need not be the sole responsibility of the federal or state governments; efforts can be made in all segments of the early childhood delivery system—from publicly funded child care centers to private, for-profit programs—to meet the needs of working parents of handicapped children.

Working parents of all children share a common problem—finding affordable, quality child care—but parents of handicapped children face additional roadblocks in their search for services. Many centers won't accept handicapped children because their staff members are not trained to care for them or they are simply frightened by the prospect.

Adding to the child care shortage is the recent liability insurance crisis that has caused many centers to shut down for lack of coverage or jack up tuition to cover the cost of soaring insurance premiums.

Meanwhile, the need for child care grows more urgent. In 1986, 48 percent of mothers with children under age 6 were in the workforce, 33 percent of them working full time, according to the American Enterprise Institute. By 1995, the number of preschool-age children with working mothers will grow by 35 percent, the Children's Defense Fund predicts.

While child care for handicapped children is not widespread, there are innovative programs around the country that can be used as models for coordinating public funds and training personnel.

Delaware

Three independent efforts are under way in Delaware. The state is designing a program to train family day care providers to work with handicapped children, a private child care agency is setting up a referral service for parents of handicapped children, and a private corporation is opening a full-day child care program for both handicapped and nonhandicapped preschoolers.

The University of Delaware, under a Handicapped Children's Early Education Program grant from the U.S. Education Department, will train family day care providers — a group that, in their homes, provides the bulk of the nation's child care — to serve handicapped infants from birth through age 2.

The university is developing a 16-hour training program to teach family day care providers about normal and atypical development and how to devise appropriate curricula for handicapped children. After training, university staff will visit providers twice a month to offer technical assistance and answer questions about serving handicapped children.

In requesting the grant, the university was "looking at the needs of the whole family," said Linda Whitehead, project coordinator for the Delaware FIRST (Family Infant Resource Supplement and Training) program. "When an infant makes progress, sometimes it's at the sacrifice" of family members, who must arrange their schedules around the child's program, she said.

Trainees pay a $75 fee and can attend sessions either during the day or at night at local sites arranged by the university. The university pays for child care substitutes for providers who choose to learn during the day. The program started in October 1986, and staff expect to begin training providers in March 1987.

To recruit applicants, the university asked social service agencies — including the agency responsible for child care licensing — to tell the state's licensed family day care providers about the training program.

* * *

The Child Care Connection, a private, nonprofit child care information and referral agency that serves the Wilmington, Del., area, has devised a plan to match parents of handicapped preschoolers with available child care and hook up family day care providers with the University of Delaware's training program.

About one third of Delaware's 100 child care centers and 340 family day care providers have said they are interested in serving handicapped children, according to Paula Breen, manager of the agency.

The agency addressed child care for handicapped children at the request of parents, Breen said. "All you have to do is encounter one parent who's been clobbered by the system and you want to help."

Roberta Walker, special education supervisor for the Red Clay School District in Wilmington, encouraged the agency to pursue the issue. Her concern was aroused, she said, when she realized parents of handicapped children had no central agency they could turn to for lists of appropriate child care facilities. "Who has the time to identify these resources?" she asked.

Walker would like the agency to notify physicians, who often are the first to identify handicaps in children, about their resources for child care options.

* * *

Another gap in Delaware's child care services will be filled by a private allied health group. Occupational Physical Therapy (OPT) Services, a private allied health corporation, was to open in April 1987 a full-day child care program that will serve the needs of both handicapped and nonhandicapped preschoolers.

OPT Services, which began as a health service for handicapped preschoolers, is expanding to a full-time child care center in response to parents' needs, said Lynn Atz, OPT Services business manager.

Many parents wanted their handicapped children to receive more than just physical or occupational therapy a few hours a week, said Atz. "They wanted their children to be exposed to [nonhandicapped] children for a social experience. We looked around at [neighboring] day care centers, but nobody responded, so we decided to go ahead and do it by ourselves," she said.

Because Delaware mandates services for handicapped preschoolers starting at age 3, younger children had no opportunity for organized interaction with their nonhandicapped peers, Atz said.

At a start-up cost of $60,000, OPT Services will operate the Discovery Preschool/Daycare from 6:30 a.m. to 6 p.m., five days a week, to accommodate working parents. They already have hired a child care director and will teach staff how to develop appropriate activities for handicapped children from birth through age 3.

The program will operate as a preschool in the morning and offer child care until parents pick their children up in the evening. Therapy also will be offered to handicapped children and will be billed to the family's insurer, Atz said.

Without even advertising, Atz said, the response rate has been strong. Fifteen toddlers are enrolled, seven of them handicapped. OPT Services will charge tuition of $280 a month for children older than 15 months and $300 a month for children from birth to about 15 months, or when they can walk, she said.

Depending on the success of the program, OPT Services may expand from serving mildly and moderately handicapped children to serving severely handicapped children, Atz said.

Pennsylvania

In 1982 the Children's Development Center in Quakertown, Pa., expanded its special education program for handicapped children to accommodate the schedules of working parents and also started serving nonhandicapped preschoolers, according to Susan Lewert-Harlan, the center's executive director.

Researching the needs of working parents, the center in 1982 approached local child care centers about offering services for its handicapped children. "When we talked to the local day care centers, they were not real receptive to taking our kids, so we gradually started to extend our hours," Lewert-Harlan said.

In 1987 the program serves children from 7:45 a.m to 5:15 p.m. and is supported by a variety of funding sources. The center now accepts children subsidized by federal child care funds for low-income families and also receives support from the state mental health/mental retardation and education departments and the United Way.

Tuition varies according to the child's eligibility for public funds, Lewert-Harlan said. Low-income nonhandicapped children referred to the center receive full federal child care support. Low-income handicapped children receive federal support for the child care portion of the day, and the center refers them to the state mental health/mental retardation department for funds to pay for four hours a day of speech and language therapy. Families of handicapped children that do not qualify for federal child care support must pay $1 an hour for each hour of child care received after the four-hour therapy session. The center serves children from birth to age 5 and offers child care to children starting at 18 months.

St. Louis, Missouri

In St. Louis, Mo., the Affton and Lindbergh school districts have collaborated to provide extended-day services that integrate mildly and moderately handicapped preschoolers and their nonhandicapped peers.

The program operates from 6:30 a.m. to 6 p.m. for 3- and 4-year-old handicapped and nonhandicapped children, according to Sheila Sherman, director of the districts' early childhood program. The integrated extended-day classes, along with half-day preschool classes for handicapped preschoolers, are housed in a former junior high school building.

The program is tuition-based because Missouri's mandate to serve handicapped and nonhandicapped children starts at age 5, with no entitlement to serve preschoolers. "But the community needs good education and good child care, so the districts are offering it," Sherman said.

Tuition for all children is $62 a week for a full week. The program uses funds from the Education for All Handicapped Children Act, P.L. 94-142, to pay for related health therapy for handicapped children, she said.

Certified early childhood special educators work with the handicapped children in the integrated classroom for three to six hours a week. But because Missouri does not mandate preschool education, the school operates under the state child care licensing regulations, which do not require general preschool teachers to be certified. "We try to have one person in each classroom with some education degree, but it's not really mandatory," Sherman said.

Vermont

Vermont is committed to developing a child care plan as part of its state early childhood planning grant. To extend child care services to handicapped children, the state is considering expanding its state-supported child care program beyond the low-income population it currently serves to assist special needs families of any income, said Kristin Hawkes Reedy, an early education consultant to the Vermont education department's division of special and compensatory education.

The state also hopes to tap the expertise of the special education community to train child care providers to work with handicapped preschoolers, Reedy added. A public school special educator could supervise a child care center and ensure that handicapped children's school-determined individualized education programs (IEPs) are being properly executed by trained child care professionals, she said.

"My sense is that" child care providers are interested in serving handicapped preschoolers, but they are "concerned about meeting the needs of really severely handicapped kids," Reedy said.

Financial responsibility in this coordinated effort is still unclear. Like many states, Vermont has not determined whether the public schools should pay child care tuition above the special education and health therapy they would offer the child, she said.

* * *

As more parents enter the workforce and place their children with outside caretakers, child care becomes an increasingly vital service without which families of young handicapped children could be paralyzed.

As states create or adapt developmental programs for handicapped infants, toddlers and preschoolers, they are in a position to incorporate child care services in their plans. States have a valuable opportunity to train child care providers not only to work with handicapped children but also to foster their development.

From Our Rolodex

Kristin Hawkes Reedy
Essential Early Education
 Consultant
Vermont Department of Education
120 State St.
Montpelier, Vt. 05602
(802)828-3141

Susan Lewert-Harlan
Executive Director
Children's Development Program
P.O. Box 8
Quakertown, Pa. 18951
(215)536-8359

Linda Whitehead
Project Coordinator
Delaware FIRST
Department of Infant and
 Family Studies
Newark, Del. 19716
(302)451-6617

Sheila Sherman
Director of Early Childhood
12225 Edie and Park St.
St. Louis, Mo. 63126
(314)842-3050

Case Study 5.1

Program: **Extended Day Care Project, Madison, Wis.**

Summary: The project sends resource teachers into child care centers or family day care homes that serve both handicapped and nonhandicapped students. The aim is to train the providers to ensure the handicapped child's successful participation in the program.

Contacts: **1.** Karin Bachman, project director, Extended Day Care Project, United Cerebral Palsy of Greater Dane County, 5902 Raymond Road, Madison, Wis. 53711, (608)273-3318
2. Barbara Hoffman, Purple Crayon Family Day Care, 146 Belmont Road, Madison, Wis. 53714, (608)241-8698

Barbara Hoffman spends eight hours every weekday in her home with up to eight children. Three are hers; the others, including two handicapped children, are deposited at Hoffman's Purple Crayon Family Day Care by their parents.

Hoffman works alone, so she misses the adult companionship she had when she worked in a child care center before having her first child in 1982. And eight children can be a handful, especially when two have special needs that can take time away from her own children.

That's where the Extended Day Care Project fits in. Run out of the offices of United Cerebral Palsy in Madison, Wis., the project gives Hoffman the support and encouragement she needs to open her home to handicapped children and deal creatively with the challenges they pose.

"Sometimes I have questions, sometimes I feel frustrated," said Hoffman, an early childhood education specialist. A resource teacher from Extended Day Care spends three hours once a week at Hoffman's home, letting her "really bounce off my feelings," Hoffman said. "They can give me suggestions. They can let me know if I'm heading in the right direction. I think that's really helped me keep going."

The weekly visit has more concrete effects as well. Hoffman plans activities that couldn't take place without an extra adult to lend a hand, either something messy such as fingerpainting or a field trip such as going to the zoo.

The other side of the service Extended Day Care provides is to parents of handicapped children, finding them people like Hoffman—or, for older children, child care centers—that are willing to take handicapped children.

The project began a decade ago in response to parents in the Madison, Wis., area, who were complaining to social service agencies that "they had trouble finding day care and having their children mainstreamed into family day care," said Karin Bachman, project director for the Extended Day Care Project.

"We help parents sort through the hundreds" of area child care providers so they don't have to make phone calls to places that don't accept handicapped children, said Bachman. The project has a list of those who have expressed interest in taking children with special needs, and one of its main goals is to encourage more child care providers to take handicapped children, she said. The project also keeps records and can give parents such information as what a certain center's certification is, how many children they can take, what their philosophy is and what their hours and fees are.

The project looks for child care placement for handicapped children from birth to age 18. In early 1987, the project was serving 30 children in 20 centers or family day care homes, Bachman said. It has six resource teachers.

"The main part of our job is educating the people who run day care centers," said Bachman. "Our primary goal is to open centers to handicapped children" and to ensure their staff is better qualified to handle children with special needs.

The project provides inservice training to child care staff. For instance, to help a center serve a nonverbal child with cerebral palsy who is in a wheelchair, the resource teachers would go over the goals for the child, spell out special feeding needs or behavioral concerns and physically demonstrate how to feed the child or reposition him in the wheelchair. The resource teacher also will let the child care staff know how things are going at home for the child, and if the child is of school age, what the child is working on in school.

The goal, said Bachman, is for the resource teachers to gradually decrease the amount of time they spend at a child care center. "We say, 'We'll be here until you feel comfortable.' With some kids, we provide full-time resources and it's never decreased. With most kids, it's not that long," she said. Bachman said it would be impossible to estimate an average, but noted that for some children it's less than a month. "Some children adjust so easily, and their needs are fairly minimal."

Bachman said the child care providers she works with do not differentiate between handicapped and nonhandicapped children in fees, and, indeed, Hoffman charges the same price, $1.75 an hour, for all children, regardless of age or needs.

Placements for younger children tend to be in family day care homes such as Hoffman's because they typically function better in smaller groups. Hoffman's charges range in age from 1 to 6.

Another project goal is to help educate the nonhandicapped children, telling them "how this [handicapped] child is the same as you are, or a very simple explanation of the child's needs," Bachman said. "Gradually that becomes something you don't have to work out, after the child has been there for a while."

Hoffman believes the integration has worked well for both the handicapped and nonhandicapped children. "It's really good for them [the nonhandicapped children] to be with kids of special needs so they can see that everyone is different. They learn to accept children as what they are at an early age. Hopefully, that will carry on to a later age."

At one time, Hoffman said, she took care of a 4-year-old girl with cerebral palsy who could not walk, but just pulled herself along on the floor. The other children "copied what she did. For a while, they all crawled on the floor," Hoffman said. "They experimented with what it would be like to crawl, to not be able to walk. The kids were real sympathetic to her feelings. It was really neat, they saw through the whole thing that she's a person like them with feelings."

Taking other children into her home benefits her children in other ways, Hoffman said. "They really look forward to the other kids coming. On weekends, they ask why I don't take care of other children. Because I take care of other children, I do more child-oriented activities than if I were a homemaker. It's nice for them. They have built-in playmates."

Chapter Six

Parents: An Increasingly Powerful Role

If there's one thing everyone agrees on about P.L. 99-457, it's that the law gives parents a much larger say in the design of their child's education.

The law "does a lot to strengthen parents," said Martha Ziegler, who runs the Technical Assistance for Parent Programs (TAPP) Project through a U.S. Education Department contract. "The law starts much earlier to empower parents and should positively affect the role of parents. Parents will really be included as partners."

The new program for infants and toddlers is based on a case management approach, in which working with the family is an integral part of serving the child. Each family must have a written individualized family service plan (IFSP) developed by a multidisciplinary team that includes the parent or guardian. The plan is to be evaluated once a year and reviewed at least every six months.

IFSPs must contain information on the child's level of development, the family's strengths and needs, the outcomes expected, the services needed, the date services will begin and their expected duration, the name of the case manager, and how to help the child make the transition to services provided for 3-year-olds if appropriate. In their focus on the family, IFSPs go beyond the individualized education programs (IEPs) required under the Education for All Handicapped Children Act, P.L. 94-142, for children age 3 and older.

Congress also supported increased parental participation in programs for 3- through 5-year-olds. The House Education and Labor Committee noted that the family is considered the "primary learning environment" for children under age 6, citing testimony that called for parents and professionals to work together. Thus, the panel said in its report accompanying the bill that became P.L. 99-457, Congress "expects that whenever appropriate and to the extent desired by the parents the preschooler's IEP will include instruction for parents so that they can be active and knowledgeable in assisting their child's progress."

The increased emphasis on parents "represents an awareness of Congress that families and parents have a key stake and role in this whole notion of comprehensive services—the family as being not only recipients of services but also as drivers of the systems of services for themselves—so that they have an opportunity to direct and to be involved in what will be best for their children and themselves," said Pascal Trohanis, director of the State Technical Assistance Resource Team (START) at the University of North Carolina's Frank Porter Graham Child Development Center in Chapel Hill.

Since Congress enacted P.L. 94-142 in 1975, parents of handicapped children have grown increasingly influential. A grassroots effort by parents and advocates in 1982 was largely credited with halting a U.S. Education Department attempt to deregulate P.L. 94-142.

The 1983 Education of the Handicapped Act Amendments enhanced the role of parents by establishing a system of grants to support organized parent-to-parent information and training programs. TAPP is the technical assistance arm of the system, which provides grants to those programs, run by Parent Training and Information Centers nationwide (for a list of the centers, see Appendix F).

The gradual progress and increasing awareness by professionals of the key role parents play in their children's development may have led to the even stronger parental role in P.L. 99-457, said Ziegler. "One of the things I find very encouraging is the fact that a lot of leading professionals around the country are pushing hard for a strong role for parents," she said. "I'm inclined to think [P.L.] 94-142 may have helped professionals come to an understanding that it's important for parents to have a different role and a better role early on. They may now be aware of how unaware parents often are when children reach school age."

Before the federal government backed concrete parent involvement by funding the parent centers, "parents had to rely on the grapevine, one parent tells another and so forth," said Charlotte DesJardins, who runs the Coordinating Council for Handicapped Children in Chicago.

DesJardins sees the establishment of the IFSPs as "very positive," adding, "If you don't have the parent involved, the child isn't going to progress. This is more true of handicapped children than any other child. Parents have to be involved with the agency as partners, not just as implementors of other people's decisions. They need to be involved in the decisionmaking process itself."

Ultimately, she added, parental involvement helps the child. "I have found that when people have been involved and when they understand the reason for something, they are much more willing to cooperate and are eager to cooperate," she said. "Most parents want to do right by their kids. What interferes is they don't know what is best."

Stages Of Grief

Researchers support that point of view. Particularly with newborns, it is critical that parents learn what works best with their child's handicap, for only then can progress be made, said Dr. T. Berry Brazelton, a leading early intervention researcher who is chief of the child development unit at Boston Children's Hospital.

Parents of a handicapped baby go through all the stages of grieving experienced in the unexpected loss of a loved one. They feel shock and despair, they deny the handicap exists and they act detached, said Brazelton. These reactions are normal, and educators and other professionals who work with parents need to understand how to work through them, he wrote in "Early Intervention: What Does It Mean?," an article published in the journal *Theory and Research in Behavioral Pediatrics*.

Brazelton, who also is a professor of pediatrics at Harvard Medical School, explained, for instance, that "the caring mother, who feels she has already damaged the infant, feels also that if she were out of the way or detached the infant might be less at risk. This serves to make her less available to the infant."

But professionals must work with parents to show them their involvement is critical to the infant's progress, he wrote. "Even in the face of a devastating diagnosis of retardation in the baby, a parent can have the energy available to search for and work with the baby's more hopeful, positive behavior." Unless parents can turn their grieving around, Brazelton wrote, "the parent can remain permanently withdrawn and unavailable to an at-risk child. The job of intervention is to *accept* the negative forces of grieving, but to work to free positive forces for interaction with the child as well."

Monitoring And Education

The increased role of parents means an increased responsibility as well, said DesJardins; that is, a responsibility to help monitor programs and to continue to educate parents.

"As soon as you give people money, that's a big incentive right there to start a program," said DesJardins. "We'll need proper monitoring of how the programs are being implemented, that you don't just have a lot of people who put together a pot of money just to fulfill the letter of the law. We're going to need to be very conscious of that and monitor the situation," along with nonprofit organizations, professionals, service providers and federal, state and local government.

It's key, she said, that parent education reach out to all parents, not just the already motivated middle class. "I have found, in doing training in public housing projects and a lot of other places, that minority populations are terribly underestimated. Their intelligence is underestimated, their skills are underestimated, their coping skills and their capabilities are terribly underestimated."

Parent projects are slowly beginning to reach out to another under-involved group, teenage mothers, said Winifred Anderson, executive director of the Parent Educational Advocacy Training Center in Alexandria, Va. As discussed in Case Study 2.1, children of adolescent mothers are likely to be at risk of developmental delays, and the mothers themselves have unique biological and social problems that must be addressed for them to adequately rear their children.

And it is urgent that all parents be educated because "children whose parents do have some access and take advantage of some training programs for parents are ones who have a better chance of improved growth and development," said Anderson, whose agency serves parents in Virginia, Maryland and West Virginia.

To implement the new law, she said, "I sense an intensifying of the efforts school systems are going to need to put forth. I think many school systems have come a long way over the years, yet this is a very new area for them, the very young children and their parents. There are issues that are different. So I think the role for parent information and training centers is just going to be vital, to really assist the school system" in putting the new programs in place.

Much educating of parents comes from the parent centers, which provide a wide variety of education services, including actual classes and individual consultations.

To illustrate, Anderson's center provides individual consultation services that include review of school records, explanation of school evaluations and test results, help in preparing and monitoring the IEP, classroom observation to assess placement, and preparation for and assistance at administrative proceedings. Fees are charged on a sliding scale.

In addition, the center offers a seven-hour introductory course on the role of parents in special education, a 15-hour course that prepares parents to be effective advocates for their children's educational needs, and another 15-hour course that teaches parents the skills needed to help their children get vocational training. A four-day course teaches parents to teach the shorter courses to their peers.

Other educating comes from the programs for children, which understand the pressing need for family training, especially in the early years of life. One of many such programs is Project Enlightenment in Raleigh, N.C., which trains families in parenting techniques and play therapy (see Case Study 6.1).

"It's a good thing that the government recognizes the benefit that families are going to reap from it," said DesJardins. "There are obvious monetary benefits to the government as well. The earlier families are brought into the act, the more benefit to society. Children are going to be able to do a lot more, be more employable. This is not an altruistic thing on the part of the government. It's a damn good investment."

From Our Rolodex

Winifred Anderson
Executive Director
Parent Educational Advocacy Training Center
228 S. Pitt St., Suite 300
Alexandria, Va. 22314
(703)836-2953

Charlotte DesJardins
Coordinating Council for Handicapped Children
20 E. Jackson Blvd., Room 900
Chicago, Ill. 60604
(312)939-3513

Martha Ziegler
TAPP Project
312 Stuart St.
Boston, Mass. 02116
(617)482-2915

Case Study 6.1

Program: Project Enlightenment, Raleigh, N.C.

Summary: Project Enlightenment is an early intervention program designed to enhance the social and emotional development of children by training their families in parenting techniques and play therapy.

Contacts: 1. Alice Burrows, director, Project Enlightenment, 501 Boylan Ave., Raleigh, N.C. 27603, (919)755-6935
2. Dr. Tom Haizlip, director, Child and Youth Services, Dorothea Dix Hospital, 820 S. Boylan Ave., Raleigh, N.C. 27611, (919)733-5344
3. Karen Ponder, director, St. James Preschool, 3808 New Hope Road, Raleigh, N.C. 27604, (919)876-8939

David and Carol Miller-Smith were not prepared for all the changes that accompanied their move to Raleigh, N.C. There was David's new job, remodeling their new house, and preschool for their 3-year-old son, Zack. And then there was the news that came one morning in a phone call from Zack's teacher.

Zack was having problems in class, the teacher said. He played alone and had trouble socializing with other children. He often didn't pay attention in class and displayed impulsive behavior on the playground. The teacher recommended counseling.

"That was a real painful time for us because we just didn't know what was happening. This was our first born," said Carol.

With little knowledge of the area and no idea where to turn for help, the Miller-Smiths followed the recommendation of Zack's preschool. They turned to Project Enlightenment, an organization that offers a wide range of support services to families and preschool professionals.

That was nearly three years ago. Today Zack is in a self-contained class for exceptional children in the Wake County, N.C., schools. Although he has problems with motor skills and continues to have difficulty writing, he is doing well in his academic work. "He actually taught himself to read when he was 4-years-old," said Carol.

She credits Project Enlightenment for showing her and David how to build on Zack's strengths and help him overcome his weaknesses. She is still awed by the support she received from the project staff during that critical time. "It was like moving into a womb," she said.

"We work with the family, the school and the child as a unit," Project Director Alice Burrows explained. "It is a true systems approach.

We believe that the child's environment has to change before the child can change."

Housed in a 66-year-old former elementary school in Raleigh, Project Enlightenment serves as school, library and training institution. Its 31-member staff includes early childhood education and child development specialists, social workers, psychologists, physical therapists, speech and language specialists, and special educators.

The Miller-Smiths' experience illustrates the range of services the project offers. Project specialists began by visiting Zack's preschool and observing his behavior at home. They referred him for diagnosis and evaluated his needs, finding his motor skills were about two years delayed and that he suffered from an attention deficit disorder. The specialists recommended the Miller-Smiths enroll Zack in Project Enlightenment's demonstration preschool.

Meanwhile, Carol and David worked with the specialists to learn parenting and play therapy techniques to use with Zack at home. The couple also began attending the project's parenting classes and joined one of the many parent support groups it sponsors. They often visited the project's Parent Teacher Resource Center, a service that catalogs resources on child development and provides parents with instructions, materials and equipment to make toys and games for their handicapped children.

Finally, as Zack prepared to enter school, project specialists made recommendations to the Raleigh school system on his placement and advised his parents on how to deal with placement procedures in the future. For all these services the Miller-Smiths paid only $20 fees to enroll in the project's parenting classes and the costs of publications and materials for the toys and games they made.

Project Enlightenment was "a great help to us," said Carol Miller-Smith. "I wish there were more programs like it. It would save parents a lot of pain. Even for a normal child, to have someone professional identify strengths and weaknesses is really a help for a parent," she said.

In fact, the project's services are available to parents of nonhandicapped children. "We feel if we can get to the parents early, and they're promoting strong mental health in their children, then we're going to see fewer problems down the line," said Burrows.

The project's resource center and parenting classes are open to any parent or teacher seeking reference materials on child development. The demonstration preschool each year serves 10 nonhandicapped children as well as 10 handicapped children.

Project Enlightenment also sponsors for-credit courses for child care professionals, serves as a training site for child psychiatry residents at the University of North Carolina Medical School in Raleigh and conducts with Wake Memorial Hospital a program called "First Years Together." First Years identifies high-risk infants at birth and offers counseling and diagnostic services to their families before their children leave the hospital.

"TalkLine," the project's phone-in service, is staffed six hours a week to answer parents' questions about their children's behavior. The service has operated since 1979.

The project's activities have evolved and expanded since its founding in 1969 as a child guidance clinic. At that time, North Carolina offered no kindergarten services, and Raleigh school officials were alarmed at the number of children having problems in the first grade. At the same time, Dr. Tom Haizlip, then director of the child psychiatry training program at Dorothea Dix Hospital in Raleigh, was interested in developing a field training program.

Haizlip, while working on a contract with the Raleigh and Wake County schools to determine the levels of preschool education among children entering the first grade, saw an opportunity to meet everyone's needs. With the help of the school systems and the Wake County Mental Health Center, he applied for and got a $300,000, three-year grant from the U.S. Education Department to establish a child guidance clinic in Raleigh.

"I think the reason behind the program's endurance is its willingness to adapt," said Haizlip, who now is director of child and youth services at the Dorothea Dix Hospital in Raleigh and continues to serve as a consultant to the project and use it as a training site for child psychiatrists.

"This is the only service where we [private preschools] are actually in touch with the public school system," said Karen Ponder, director of St. James Preschool in Raleigh.

"Our staff works with Project Enlightenment. Our parents work with them [project specialists] and they work with our children," she said.

St. James was one of five Raleigh preschools that cooperated with the project in its first year of operation in 1969. At the time, said Burrows, many area preschools were reluctant to invite project specialists to observe their programs because "they were afraid we were evaluating them and afraid they would be closed if we didn't like what they were doing."

To calm their fears, Project Enlightenment staff enlisted the help of five schools to demonstrate to the others that their program was a support service—not a threat. "We went in and helped wash the dishes," Burrows said. "We cooked the lunches. We felt they could teach us about daycare," she said, "so we set it up as a mutually beneficial, cooperative relationship."

Soon teachers from other preschools began bringing their questions about children's behavior to Burrows' staff, and more and more preschools began opening their doors to Project Enlightenment.

"It just took time to help them realize we were serious about this," Burrows said, adding that even today project staff members will not enter a preschool unless they are invited.

The project currently survives on financial support from a number of agencies and organizations. "At one time," said Burrows, "we had 12 funding sources." When the original grant expired in 1972, the project turned to the National Institute of Mental Health, which supported its operations for the next eight years.

The Wake County School District, which merged with the Raleigh schools in the early 1970s, has increased its support of Project Enlightenment gradually since 1969 and currently is the program's primary sponsor. The school system contributed $375,000 of the project's $696,000 budget in the 1986- 87 school year. Other funds come from the Wake County Area Mental Health Center, the state board of education, the Raleigh Junior League and fees charged for courses, publications and materials. There also is a fee for enrollment in the demonstration preschool, but the program does offer scholarships.

Burrows said Project Enlightenment's services can be duplicated in other communities. Since its founding in 1969 it has given birth to several other early intervention and prevention programs in the state and has been cited as a model program in numerous national publications. But, Burrows said, "one big problem in getting a program going and growing is getting your financial base." It's important to go slowly and make each step successful. "That's how you get your money," she said. "If you do something successful, you can sell it. People are demanding the service, and you get more support for your service the more valuable people think it is."

Conclusion

Congress was at its altruistic best when it designed P.L. 99-457. The law sends a message to the nation that we all are responsible for meeting the developmental and health needs of the youngest handicapped children.

But, as with P.L. 94-142, the altruism ends with the passage of the law and the appropriation of federal "seed money" to help run the programs.

States are left to thrash out the logistics of financing and running new programs. The challenge is extraordinary. With limited resources, states must plan. Plan financially, plan to train a new generation of personnel to address special needs, plan to integrate handicapped preschoolers with their nonhandicapped peers, plan to change the image of public schools as no place to serve infants, and plan to have public schools and other agencies work more closely with parents.

The result could mean a revolution in education and social services for handicapped children. The process will be arduous and riddled with problems. States will have to design regulations that ensure program quality and give their agencies the flexibility to work with other early childhood service providers.

With its emphasis on interagency agreements, P.L. 99-457 presents a unique opportunity for states to fuse their fragmented early childhood services into one comprehensive system. Through clever planning, they can work with child care programs to provide the youngest handicapped children with health, education and extended-day care services. A system that facilitates communication between public schools and outside child care programs early in handicapped children's lives will also lay the groundwork for their smooth transition to kindergarten or first grade.

Perhaps the pressure to coordinate services between private and public early childhood programs will inspire states to create one set of quality standards to which all programs must adhere. Such a requirement may serve to increase the quality of early childhood services in all sectors.

P.L. 99-457 can be the springboard to reform. The choice — and the responsibility — is left to the states.

Appendices

Appendix A
Text Of P.L. 99-457

Appendix A

Education Of The Handicapped Act Amendments Of 1986 P.L. 99-457

An Act

To amend the Education of the Handicapped Act to reauthorize the discretionary programs under that Act, to authorize an early intervention program under that Act for handicapped infants and toddlers and their families, and for other purposes.

Be it enacted by the Senate and House of Representatives of the United States of America in Congress assembled,

SECTION 1, SHORT TITLE: REFERENCE.

(a) SHORT TITLE. — This Act may be cited as the "Education of the Handicapped Act Amendments of 1986."
(b) REFERENCE. — References in this Act to "the Act" and references to the Education of the Handicapped Act. *(20 USC 1400)*

TITLE I — HANDICAPPED INFANTS AND TODDLERS

SEC. 101. ADDITION OF A NEW PART RELATING TO HANDICAPPED INFANTS AND TODDLERS.

(a) AMENDMENT. — The Act is amended by inserting after the part added by section 316 the following new part:

"PART H — HANDICAPPED INFANTS AND TODDLERS

"FINDINGS AND POLICY

"SEC. 671. (a) FINDINGS. — The Congress finds that there is an urgent and substantial need — *(20 USC 1471)*
"(1) to enhance the development of handicapped infants and toddlers and to minimize their potential for developmental delay,
"(2) to reduce the educational costs to our society, including our Nation's schools, by minimizing the need for special education and related services after handicapped infants and toddlers reach school age,
"(3) to minimize the likelihood of institutionalization of handicapped individuals and maximize the potential for their independent living in society, and

"(4) to enhance the capacity of families to meet the special needs of their infants and toddlers with handicaps.

"(b) POLICY.—It is therefore the policy of the United States to provide financial assistance to States—

"(1) to develop and implement a statewide, comprehensive, coordinated, multidisciplinary, interagency program of early intervention services for handicapped infants and toddlers and their families,

"(2) to facilitate the coordination of payment for early intervention services from Federal, State, local, and private sources (including public and private insurance coverage), and

"(3) to enhance its capacity to provide quality early intervention services and expand and improve existing early intervention services being provided to handicapped infants, toddlers, and their families.

"DEFINITIONS

"SEC. 672. As used in this part—*(20 USC 1472)*

"(1) The term 'handicapped infants and toddlers' means individuals from birth to age 2, inclusive, who need early intervention services because they—

"(A) are experiencing developmental delays, as measured by appropriate diagnostic instruments and procedures in one or more of the following areas: Cognitive development, physical development, language and speech development, psychosocial development, or self-help skills, or

"(B) have a diagnosed physical or mental condition which has a high probability of resulting in developmental delay.

Such term may also include, at a State's discretion, individuals from birth to age 2, inclusive, who are at risk of having substantial developmental delays if early intervention services are not provided.

"(2) 'Early intervention services' are developmental services which—

"(A) are provided under public supervision,

"(B) are provided at no cost except where Federal or State law provides for a system of payments by families, including a schedule of sliding fees,

"(C) are designed to meet a handicapped infant's or toddler's developmental needs in any one or more of the following areas:

"(i) physical development,
"(ii) cognitive development,
"(iii) language and speech development,
"(iv) psycho-social development, or
"(v) self-help skills,

"(D) meet the standards of the State, including the requirements of this part,
"(E) include—
"(i) family training, counseling, and home visits,
"(ii) special instruction,
"(iii) speech pathology and audiology,
"(iv) occupational therapy,
"(v) physical therapy,
"(vi) psychological services,
"(vii) case management services,
"(viii) medical services only for diagnostic or evaluation purposes,
"(ix) early identification, screening, and assessment services, and
"(x) health services necessary to enable the infant or toddler to benefit from the other early intervention services,
"(F) are provided by qualified personnel, including—
"(i) special educators,
"(ii) speech and language pathologists and audiologists,
"(iii) occupational therapists,
"(iv) physical therapists,
"(v) psychologists,
"(vi) social workers,
"(vii) nurses, and
"(viii) nutritionists, and
"(G) are provided in conformity with an individualized family service plan adopted in accordance with section 677.
"(3) The term 'developmental delay' has the meaning given such term by a State under section 676(b)(1).
"(4) The term 'Council' means the State Interagency Coordinating Council established under section 682.

"GENERAL AUTHORITY

"SEC. 673. The Secretary shall, in accordance with this part, make grants to States (from their allocations under section 684) to assist each State to develop a statewide, comprehensive, coordinated, multidisciplinary, interagency system to provide early intervention services for handicapped infants and toddlers and their families. *(20 USC 1473)*

"GENERAL ELIGIBILITY

"SEC. 674. In order to be eligible for a grant under section 673 for any fiscal year, a State shall demonstrate to the Secretary (in its application under section 678) that the State has established a State Interagency Coordinating Council which meets the requirements of section 682. *(20 USC 1474)*

"CONTINUING ELIGIBILITY

"SEC. 675. (a) FIRST TWO YEARS. — In order to be eligible for a grant under section 673 for the first or second year of a State's participation under this part, a State shall include in its application under section 678 for that year assurances that funds received under section 673 shall be used to assist the State to plan, develop, and implement the statewide system required by section 676. *(20 USC 1475)*

"(b) THIRD AND FOURTH YEAR. — (1) In order to be eligible for a grant under section 673 for the third or fourth year of a State's participation under this part, a State shall include in its application under 678 for that year information and assurances demonstrating to the satisfaction of the Secretary that—

"(A) the State has adopted a policy which incorporates all of the components of a statewide system in accordance with section 676 or obtained a waiver from the Secretary under paragraph (2),

"(B) funds shall be used to plan, develop, and implement the statewide system required by section 676, and

"(C) such statewide system will be in effect no later than the beginning of the fourth year of the State's participation under section 673, except that with respect to section 676(b)(4), a State need only conduct multidisciplinary assessments, develop individualized family service plans, and make available case management services.

"(2) Notwithstanding paragraph (1), the Secretary may permit a State to continue to receive assistance under section 673 during such third year even if the State has not adopted the policy required by paragraph (1)(A) before receiving assistance if the State demonstrates in its application—

"(A) that the State has made a good faith effort to adopt such a policy,

"(B) the reasons why it was unable to meet the timeline and the steps remaining before such a policy will be adopted, and

"(C) an assurance that the policy will be adopted and go into effect before the fourth year of such assistance.

"(c) FIFTH AND SUCCEEDING YEARS. — In order to be eligible for a grant under section 673 for a fifth and any succeeding year of a State's participation under this part, a State shall include in its application under section 678 for that year information and assurances demonstrating to the satisfaction of the Secretary that the State has in effect the statewide system required by section 676 and a description of services to be provided under section 676(b)(2).

"(d) EXCEPTION. — Notwithstanding subsections (a) and (b), a State which has in effect a State law, enacted before September 1, 1986, that requires the provision of free appropriate public education to handicapped children from birth through age 2, inclusive, shall be eligible for a grant under section 673 for the first through fourth years of a State's participation under this part.

"REQUIREMENTS FOR STATEWIDE SYSTEM

"SEC. 676. (a) IN GENERAL. — A statewide system of coordinated, comprehensive, multidisciplinary, interagency programs providing appropriate early intervention services to all handicapped infants and toddlers and their families shall include the minimum components under subsection (b). *(20 USC 1476)*

"(b) MINIMUM COMPONENTS. — The statewide system required by subsection (a) shall include, at a minimum —
 "(1) a definition of the term 'developmentally delayed' that will be used by the State in carrying out programs under this part,
 "(2) timetables for ensuring that appropriate early intervention services will be available to all handicapped infants and toddlers in the State before the beginning of the fifth year of a State's participation under this part,
 "(3) a timely, comprehensive, multidisciplinary evaluation of the functioning of each handicapped infant and toddler in the State and the needs of the families to appropriately assist in the development of the handicapped infant or toddler,
 "(4) for each handicapped infant and toddler in the State, an individualized family service plan in accordance with section 677, including case management services in accordance with such service plan,
 "(5) a comprehensive child find system, consistent with part B, including a system for making referrals to service providers that includes timelines and provides for the participation by primary referral sources,
 "(6) a public awareness program focusing on early identification of handicapped infants and toddlers,
 "(7) a central directory which includes early intervention services, resources, and experts available in the State and research and demonstration projects being conducted in the State,
 "(8) a comprehensive system of personnel development,
 "(9) a single line of responsibility in a lead agency designated or established by the Governor for carrying out —
  "(A) the general administration, supervision, and monitoring of programs and activities receiving assistance under section 673 to ensure compliance with this part,
  "(B) the identification and coordination of all available

resources within the State from Federal, State, local and private sources,

"(C) the assignment of financial responsibility to the appropriate agency,

"(D) the development of procedures to ensure that services are provided to handicapped infants and toddlers and their families in a timely manner pending the resolution of any disputes among public agencies or service providers,

"(E) the resolution of intra- and interagency disputes, and

"(F) the entry into formal interagency agreements that define the financial responsibility of each agency for paying for early intervention services (consistent with State law) and procedures for resolving disputes and that include all additional components necessary to ensure meaningful cooperation and coordination,

"(10) a policy pertaining to the contracting or making of other arrangements with service providers to provide early intervention services in the State, consistent with the provisions of this part, including the contents of the application used and the conditions of the contract or other arrangements,

"(11) a procedure for securing timely reimbursement of funds used under this part in accordance with section 681(a),

"(12) procedural safeguards with respect to programs under this part as required by section 680, and

"(13) policies and procedures relating to the establishment and maintenance of standards to ensure that personnel necessary to carry out this part are appropriately and adequately prepared and trained, including—

"(A) the establishment and maintenance of standards which are consistent with any State approved or recognized certification, licensing, registration, or other comparable requirements which apply to the area in which such personnel are providing early intervention services, and

"(B) to the extent such standards are not based on the highest requirements in the State applicable to a specific profession or discipline, the steps the State is taking to require the retraining or hiring of personnel that meet appropriate professional requirements in the State, and

"(14) a system for compiling data on the numbers of handicapped infants and toddlers and their families in the State in need of appropriate early intervention services (which may be based on a sampling of data), the numbers of such infants and toddlers and their families served, the types of services provided (which may be based on a sampling of data), and other information required by the Secretary.

"INDIVIDUALIZED FAMILY SERVICE PLAN

SEC. 677. (a) ASSESSMENT AND PROGRAM DEVELOPMENT. — Each handicapped infant or toddler and the infant or toddler's family will receive — *(20 USC 1477)*

"(1) a multidisciplinary assessment to unique needs and the identification of services appropriate to meet such needs, and

"(2) a written individualized family service plan developed by a multidisciplinary team, including the parent or guardian, as required by subsection (d).

"(b) PERIODIC REVIEW. — The individualized family service plan shall be evaluated once a year and the family shall be provided a review of the plan at 6 month-intervals (or more often where appropriate based on infant and toddler and family needs).

"(c) PROMPTNESS AFTER ASSESSMENT. — The individualized family service plan shall be developed within a reasonable time after the assessment required by subsection (a)(1) is completed. With the parent's consent, early intervention services may commence prior to the completion of such assessment.

"(d) CONTENT OF PLAN. — The individualized family service plan shall be in writing and contain —

"(1) a statement of the infant's or toddler's present levels of physical development, cognitive development, language and speech development, psycho-social development, and self-help skills, based on acceptable objective criteria,

"(2) a statement of the family's strengths and needs relating to enhancing the development of the family's handicapped infant or toddler,

"(3) a statement of the major outcomes expected to be achieved for the infant and toddler and the family, and the criteria, procedures, and timelines used to determine the degree to which progress toward achieving the outcomes are being made and whether modifications or revisions of the outcomes or services are necessary,

"(4) a statement of specific early intervention services necessary to meet the unique needs of the infant or toddler and the family, including the frequency, intensity, and the method of delivering services,

"(5) the projected dates for initiation of services and the anticipated duration of such services,

"(6) the name of the case manager from the profession most immediately relevant to the infant's and toddler's or family's needs who will be responsible for the implementation of the plan and coordination with other agencies and persons, and

"(7) the steps to be taken supporting the transition of the handicapped toddler to services provided under part B to the extent such services are considered appropriate. *(20 USC 1411)*

"STATE APPLICATION AND ASSURANCES

"SEC. 678. (a) APPLICATION.—Any State desiring to receive a grant under section 673 for any year shall submit an application to the Secretary at such time and in such manner as the Secretary may reasonably require by regulation. Such an application shall contain—*(20 USC 1478)*

"(1) a designation of the lead agency in the State that will be responsible for the administration of funds provided under section 673,

"(2) information demonstrating eligibility of the State under section 674,

"(3) the information or assurances required to demonstrate eligibility of the State for the particular year of participation under section 675, and

"(4)(A) information demonstrating that the State has provided (i) public hearings, (ii) adequate notice of such hearings, and (iii) an opportunity for comment to the general public before the submission of such application and before the adoption by the State of the policies described in such application, and (B) a summary of the public comments and the State's responses,

"(5) a description of the uses for which funds will be expended in accordance with this part and for the fifth and succeeding fiscal years a description of the services to be provided,

"(6) a description of the procedure used to ensure an equitable distribution of resources made available under this part among all geographic areas within the State, and

"(7) such other information and assurances as the Secretary may reasonably require by regulation.

"(b) STATEMENT OF ASSURANCES.—Any State desiring to receive a grant under section 673 shall file with the Secretary a statement at such time and in such manner as the Secretary may reasonably require by regulation. Such statement shall—

"(1) assure that funds paid to the State under section 673 will be expended in accordance with this part,

"(2) contain assurances that the State will comply with the requirements of section 681,

"(3) provide satisfactory assurance that the control of funds provided under section 673, and title to property derived therefrom, shall be in a public agency for the uses and purposes provided in this part and that a public agency will administer such funds and property.

"(4) provide for (A) making such reports in such form and containing such information as the Secretary may require to carry out the Secretary's functions under this part, and (B) keeping such records and affording such access thereto as the Secretary may find necessary to assure the correctness and verification of such reports and proper disbursement of Federal funds under this part,

"(5) provide satisfactory assurance that Federal funds made available under section 673 (A) will not be commingled with State funds, and (B) will be so used as to supplement and increase the level of State and local funds expended for handicapped infants and toddlers and their families and in no case to supplant such State and local funds,

"(6) provide satisfactory assurance that such fiscal control and fund accounting procedures will be adopted as may be necessary to assure proper disbursement of, and accounting for, Federal funds paid under section 673 to the State, and

"(7) such other information and assurances as the Secretary may reasonably require by regulation.

"(c) APPROVAL OF APPLICATION AND ASSURANCES REQUIRED.—No state may receive a grant under section 673 unless the Secretary has approved the application and statement of assurances of that state. The Secretary shall not disapprove such an application or statement of assurances unless the Secretary determines, after notice and opportunity for a hearing, that the application or statement of assurances fails to comply with the requirements of this section.

"USES OF FUNDS"

"SEC. 679. In addition to using funds provided under section 673 to plan, develop, and implement the statewide system required by section 676, a State may use such funds— *(20 USC 1479)*

"(1) for direct services for handicapped infants and toddlers that are not otherwise provided from other public or private sources, and

"(2) to expand and improve on services for handicapped infants and toddlers that are otherwise available.

"PROCEDURAL SAFEGUARDS"

"SEC. 680. The procedural safeguards required to be included in a statewide system under section 676(b)(12) shall provide, at a minimum, the following: *(20 USC 1480)*

"(1) The timely administrative resolution of complaints by parents. Any party aggrieved by the findings and decision regarding an administrative complaint shall have the right to bring a civil action with respect to the complaint, which action may be brought in any State court of competent jurisdiction or in a district court of the United States without regard to the amount in controversy. In any action brought under this paragraph, the court shall receive the records of the administrative proceedings, shall hear additional evidence at the request of a party, and, basing its decision on the preponderance of the evidence, grant such relief as the court determines is appropriate.

"(2) The right to confidentiality of personally identifiable information.

"(3) The opportunity for parents and a guardian to examine records relating to assessment, screening, eligibility determinations, and the development and implementation of the individualized family service plan.

"(4) Procedures to protect the rights of the handicapped infant and toddlers whenever the parents or guardian of the child are not known or unavailable or the child is a ward of the State, including the assignment of an individual (who shall not be an employee of the State agency providing services) to act as a surrogate for the parents or guardian.

"(5) Written prior notice to the parents or guardian of the handicapped infant or toddler whenever the State agency or service provider proposes to initiate or change or refuses to initiate or change the identification, evaluation, placement, or the provision of appropriate early intervention services to the handicapped infant or toddler.

"(6) Procedures designed to assure that the notice required by paragraph (5) fully informs the parents or guardian, in the parents' or guardian's native language, unless it clearly is not feasible to do so, of all procedures available pursuant to this section.

"(7) During the pendency of any proceeding or action involving a complaint, unless the State agency and the parents or guardian otherwise agree, the child shall continue to receive the appropriate early intervention services currently being provided or if applying for initial services shall receive the services not in dispute.

"PAYOR OF LAST RESORT

"SEC. 681. (a) NONSUBSTITUTION. — Funds provided under section 673 may not be used to satisfy a financial commitment for services which would have been paid for from another public or private source but for the enactment of this part, except that whenever considered necessary to prevent the delay in the receipt of appropriate early intervention services by the infant or toddler or family in a timely fashion, funds provided under section 673 may be used to pay the provider of services pending reimbursement from the agency which has ultimate responsibility for the payment. *(20 USC 1481)*

"(b) REDUCTION OF OTHER BENEFITS. — Nothing in this part shall be construed to permit the State to reduce medical or other assistance available or to alter eligibility under title V of the Social Security Act (relating to medicaid for handicapped infants and toddlers) within the State. *(42 USC 701, 42 USC 1396)*

"STATE INTERAGENCY COORDINATING COUNCIL

"SEC. 682. (a) ESTABLISHMENT. — (1) Any State which desires to receive financial assistance under section 673 shall establish a State Interagency Coordinating Council composed of 15 members.
(20 USC 1482)
"(2) The council and the chairperson of the Council shall be appointed by the Governor. In making appointments to the Council, the Governor shall ensure that the membership of the Council reasonably represents the population of the State.
"(b) COMPOSITION. — The council shall be composed of —
"(1) at least 3 parents of handicapped infants or toddlers or handicapped children aged 3 through 6, inclusive,
"(2) at least 3 public or private providers of early intervention services,
"(3) at least one representative from the State legislature,
"(4) at least one person involved in personnel preparation, and
"(5) other members representing each of the appropriate agencies involved in the provision of or payment for early intervention services to handicapped infants and toddlers and their families and others selected by the Governor.
"(c) MEETINGS. — The Council shall meet at least quarterly and in such places as it deems necessary. The meetings shall be publicly announced, and, to the extent appropriate, open and accessible to the general public.
"(d) MANAGEMENT AUTHORITY. — Subject to the approval of the Governor, the Council may prepare and approve a budget using funds under this part to hire staff, and obtain the services of such professional, technical, and clerical personnel as may be necessary to carry out its functions under this part.
"(e) FUNCTIONS OF COUNCIL. — The Council shall —
"(1) advise and assist the lead agency designated or established under section 676(b)(9) in the performance of the responsibilities set out in such section, particularly the identification of the sources of fiscal and other support for services for early intervention programs, assignment of financial responsibility to the appropriate agency, and the promotion of the interagency agreements,
"(2) advise and assist the lead agency in the preparation of applications and amendments thereto, and
"(3) prepare and submit an annual report to the Governor and to the Secretary on the status of early intervention programs for handicapped infants and toddlers and their families operated within the State.
"(f) CONFLICT OF INTEREST. — No member of the Council shall cast a vote on any matter which would provide direct financial benefit to that member or otherwise give the appearance of a conflict of interest under State law.

"(g) USE OF EXISTING COUNCILS. — To the extent that a State has established a Council before September 1, 1986, that is comparable to the Council described in this section, such Council shall be considered to be in compliance with this section. Within 4 years after the date the State accepts funds under section 673, such State shall establish a council that complies in full with this section.

"FEDERAL ADMINISTRATION

"SEC. 683. Sections 616, 617 and 620 shall, to the extent not inconsistent with this part, apply to the program authorized by this part, except that — *(20 USC 1483)*
   "(1) any reference to a State educational agency shall be deemed to be a reference to the State agency established or designated under section 676(b)(9), *(20 USC 1416, 1417, 1420)*
   "(2) any reference to the education of handicapped children and the education of all handicapped children and the provision of free public education to all handicapped children shall be deemed to be a reference to the provision of services to handicapped infants and toddlers in accordance with this part, and
   "(3) any reference to local educational agencies and intermediate educational agencies shall be deemed to be a reference to local service providers under this part.

"ALLOCATION OF FUNDS

"SEC. 684. (a) From the sums appropriated to carry out this part for any fiscal year, the Secretary may reserve 1 percent for payments to Guam, American Samoa, the Virgin Islands, the Republic of the Marshall Islands, the Federated State of Micronesia, the Republic of Palau, and the Commonwealth of the Northern Mariana Islands in accordance with their respective needs. *(20 USC 1484)*
   "(b)(1) The Secretary shall make payments to the Secretary of the Interior according to the need for such assistance for the provision of early intervention services to handicapped infants and toddlers and their families on reservations serviced by the elementary and secondary schools operated for Indians by the Department of the Interior. The amount of such payment for any fiscal year shall be 1.25 percent of the aggregate of the amount available to all States under this part for that fiscal year.
   "(2) The Secretary of the Interior may receive an allotment under paragraph (1) only after submitting to the Secretary an application which meets the requirements of section 678 and which is approved by the Secretary. Section 616 shall apply to any such applications. *(20 USC 1416)*
   "(c)(1) For each of the fiscal years 1987 through 1991 from the funds remaining after the reservation and payments under subsections (a) and (b), the Secretary shall allot to each State an amount

which bears the same ratio to the amount of such remainder as the number of infants and toddlers in the State bears to the number of infants and toddlers in all States, except that no State shall receive less than 0.15 percent of such remainder.

"(2) For the purpose of paragraph (1)—

"(A) the terms 'infants' and 'toddlers' mean children from birth to age 2, inclusive, and

"(B) the term 'State' does not include the jurisdictions described in subsection (a).

"(d) If any State elects not to receive its allotment under subsection (c)(1), the Secretary shall reallot, among the remaining States, amounts from such State in accordance with such subsection.

"AUTHORIZATION OF APPROPRIATIONS

"SEC. 685. There are authorized to be appropriated to carry out this part $50,000,000 for fiscal year 1987, $75,000,000 for fiscal year 1988, and such sums as may be necessary for each of the 3 succeeding fiscal years." *(20 USC 1485)*

(b) STUDY OF SERVICES; COORDINATION OF ACTIONS.—(1) The Secretary of Education and the Secretary of Health and Human Services shall conduct a joint study of Federal funding sources and services for early intervention programs currently available and shall jointly act to facilitate interagency coordination of Federal resources for such programs and to ensure that funding available to handicapped infants, toddlers, children, and youth from Federal programs, other than programs under the Education of the Handicapped Act, is not being withdrawn or reduced. *(20 USC 1485 note)*

(2) Not later than 18 months after the date of the enactment of this Act, the Secretary of Education and the Secretary of Health and Human Services shall submit a joint report to the Congress describing the findings of the study conducted under paragraph (1) and describing the joint action taken under that paragraph. *(20 USC 1400)*

TITLE II—HANDICAPPED CHILDREN AGED 3 TO 5

SEC. 201. PRE-SCHOOL GRANTS.

(a) AMENDMENT.—Section 619 of the Act (20 U.S.C. 1419) is amended to read as follows:

"PRE-SCHOOL GRANTS

"SEC. 619. (a)(1) For fiscal years 1987 through 1989 (or fiscal year 1990 if the Secretary makes a grant under this paragraph for such fiscal year) the Secretary shall make a grant to any State which—

"(A) has met the eligibility requirements of section 612, *(20 USC 1412)*

"(B) has a State plan approved under section 613, and *(20 USC 1413)*

"(C) provides special education and related services to handicapped children aged three to five, inclusive.

"(2)(A) For fiscal year 1987 the amount of a grant to a State under paragraph (1) may not exceed —

"(i) $300 per handicapped child aged three to five, inclusive, who received special education and related services in such State as determined under section 611(a)(3), or *(20 USC 1411)*

"(ii) if the amount appropriated under subsection (e) exceeds the product of $300 and the total number of handicapped children aged three to five, inclusive, who received special education and related services as determined under section 611(a)(3) —

"(I) $300 per handicapped child aged three to five, inclusive, who received special education and related services in such State as determined under section 611(a)(3), plus

"(II) an amount equal to the portion of the appropriation available after allocating funds to all States under subclause (1) (the excess appropriation) divided by the estimated increase, from the preceding fiscal year, in the number of handicapped children aged three to five, inclusive, who will be receiving special education and related services in all States multiplied by the estimated number of such children in such State.

"(B) For fiscal year 1988, funds shall be distributed in accordance with clause (i) or (ii) of paragraph (2)(A), except that the amount specified therein shall be $400 instead of $300.

"(C) For fiscal year 1989, funds shall be distributed in accordance with clause (i) or (ii) of paragraph (2)(A), except that the amount specified therein shall be $500 instead of $300.

"(D) If the Secretary makes a grant under paragraph (1) for fiscal year 1990, the amount of a grant to a State under such paragraph may not exceed $1,000 per handicapped child aged three to five, inclusive, who received special education and related services in such State as determined under section 611(a)(3). *(20 USC 1411)*

"(E) If the actual number of additional children served in a fiscal year differs from the estimate made under clause (ii)(II) of the applicable subparagraph, subparagraph (A)(ii)(II), the Secretary shall adjust (upwards or downwards) a State's allotment in the subsequent fiscal year.

"(F)(i) The amount of a grant under subparagraph (A), (B), or (C) to any State for a fiscal year may not exceed $3,800 per estimated handicapped child aged three to five, inclusive, who will be receiving or handicapped child aged three to five, inclusive, who is receiving special education and related services in such State.

"(ii) If the amount appropriated under subsection (e) for any fiscal year exceeds the amount of grants which may be made to the States for such fiscal year, the excess amount appropriated shall remain available for obligation under this section for 2 succeeding fiscal years.

"(3) To receive a grant under paragraph (1) a State shall make an application to the Secretary at such time, in such manner, and containing or accompanied by such information as the Secretary may reasonably require.

"(b)(1) For fiscal year 1990 (or fiscal year 1991 if required by paragraph (2)) and fiscal years thereafter the Secretary shall make a grant to any State which—

"(A) has met the eligibility requirements of section 612, and

"(B) has a State plan approved under section 613 which includes policies and procedures that assure the availability under the State law and practice of such State of a free appropriate public education for all handicapped children aged three to five, inclusive.

"(2) The Secretary may make a grant under paragraph (1) only for fiscal 1990 and fiscal years thereafter, except that if—

"(A) the aggregate amount that was appropriated under subsection (e) for fiscal years 1987, 1988, and 1989 was less than $656,000,000, and

"(B) the amount appropriated for fiscal year 1990 under subsection (e) is less than $306,000,000,

the Secretary may not make a grant under paragraph (1) until fiscal year 1991 and shall make a grant under subsection (a)(1) for fiscal year 1990.

"(3) The amount of any grant to any State under paragraph (1) for any fiscal year may not exceed $1,000 for each handicapped child in such State aged three to five, inclusive.

"(4) To receive a grant under paragraph (1) a State shall make an application to the Secretary at such time, in such manner and containing or accompanied by such information as the Secretary may reasonably require.

"(c)(1) For fiscal year 1987, a State which receives a grant under subsection (a)(1) shall—

"(A) distribute at least 70 percent of such grant to local educational agencies and intermediate educational units in such State in accordance with paragraph (3), except that in applying such section only handicapped children aged three to five, inclusive, shall be considered.

"(B) use not more than 25 percent of such grant for the planning and development of a comprehensive delivery system for which a grant could have been made under section 623(b) in effect through fiscal year 1987 and for direct and support services for handicapped children, and

"(C) use not more than 5 percent of such grant for administrative expenses related to the grant.

"(2) For fiscal years beginning after fiscal year 1987, a State which receives a grant under subsection (a)(1) or (b)(1) shall—

"(A) distribute at least 75 percent of such grant to local educational agencies and intermediate educational units in such State in accordance with paragraph (3), except that in applying such section only handicapped children aged three to five, inclusive, shall be considered,

"(B) use not more than 20 percent of such grant for the planning and development of a comprehensive delivery system for which a grant could have been made under section 623(b) in effect through fiscal year 1987 and for direct and support services for handicapped children, and

"(C) use not more than 5 percent of such grant for administrative expenses related to the grant.

"(3) From the amount of funds available to local educational agencies and intermediate educational units in any State under this section, each local educational agency or intermediate educational unit shall be entitled to—

"(A) an amount which bears the same ratio to the amount available under subsection (a)(2)(A)(i) or subsection (a)(2)(A)(ii)(I), as the case may be, as the number of handicapped children aged three to five, inclusive, who received special education and related services, as determined under section 611(a)(3) in such local educational agency or intermediate educational unit bears to the aggregate number of handicapped children aged three to five, inclusive, who received special education and related services in all local educational agencies and intermediate educational units in the State entitled to funds under this section, and *(20 USC 1411)*

"(B) to the extent funds are available under subsection (a)(2)(A)(ii)(II), an amount which bears the same ratio to the amount available under subsection (a)(2)(A)(ii)(II) as the estimated number of additional handicapped children aged three to five, inclusive, who will be receiving special education and related services in such local educational agency or intermediate educational unit bears to the aggregate number of handicapped children aged three to five, inclusive, who will be receiving special education and related services in all local educational agencies and intermediate educational units in the State entitled to funds under this section.

"(d) If the sums appropriated under subsection (e) for any fiscal year for making payments to States under subsection (a)(1) or (b)(1) are not sufficient to pay in full the maximum amounts which all States may receive under such subsection for such fiscal year, the maximum amounts which all States may receive under such subsection for such fiscal year shall be ratably reduced by first ratably reducing amounts computed under the excess appropriation provision of subsection (a)(2)(A)(ii)(II). If additional funds become available for making such payments for any fiscal year during which the preceding sentence is applicable, the reduced maximum amounts shall be increased on the same basis as they were reduced.

"(e) For grants under subsections (a)(1) and (b)(1) there are authorized to be appropriated such sums as may be necessary."

(b) CONFORMING AMENDMENTS —

(1) Section 611(a)(1)(A) of the Act (20 U.S.C. 1411 (a)(1)(A)) is amended to read as follows:

"(A) the number of handicapped children aged 3-5, inclusive, in a State who are receiving special education and related services as determined under paragraph (3) if the State is eligible for a grant under section 619 and the number of handicapped children aged 6-21, inclusive, in a State who are receiving special education and related services as so determined."
(20 USC 1419)

(2)(A) Section 611(g)(1) of the Act is amended by striking out "this part" each place it occurs and inserting in lieu thereof "subsection (a)."

(B) Section 611(g)(1) of the Act is amended by inserting "under subsection (h)" after "appropriated."

(C) Section 611(g)(2) of the Act is amended by striking out "this part" the first place it occurs and inserting in lieu thereof "this section."

(3) Section 611 of the Act is amended by adding at the end the following:

"(h) For grants under subsection (a) there are authorized to be appropriated such sums as may be necessary."

(c) EFFECTIVE DATE. — The amendment made by subsection (a) shall take effect with respect to the school year 1987-1988.
(20 USC 1419 note)

SEC. 202. ELIGIBILITY FOR FINANCIAL ASSISTANCE.

Part A of the Act is amended by adding at the end the following:
(20 USC 1400)

"ELIGIBILITY FOR FINANCIAL ASSISTANCE

"SEC. 609. Effective for fiscal years for which the Secretary may make grants under section 619(b)(1), no State or local educational agency or intermediate educational unit or other public institution or agency may receive a grant under parts C through G which relate exclusively to programs, projects, and activities pertaining to children aged three to five, inclusive, unless the State is eligible to receive a grant under section 619(b)(1)." *(20 USC 1408, 20 USC 1421-1454)*

SEC. 203. SHARING OF COSTS OF FREE APPROPRIATE PUBLIC EDUCATION.

(a) ELIGIBILITY FOR SECTION 611 GRANTS. — Section 612(6) of

the Act (20 U.S.C. 1412(6)) is amended by adding at the end the following:

"This paragraph shall not be construed to limit the responsibility of agencies other than educational agencies in a State from providing or paying for some or all of the costs of a free appropriate public education to be provided handicapped children in the State.

(b) STATE PLANS—

(1) Section 613(a)(9) of the Act (20 U.S.C. 1413(a)(9)) is amended to read as follows:

"(9) provide satisfactory assurance that Federal funds made available under this part (A) will not be commingled with State funds, and (B) will be so used as to supplement and increase the level of Federal, State, and local funds (including funds that are not under the direct control of State or local educational agencies) expended for special education and related services provided to handicapped children under this part and in no case to supplant such Federal, State, and local funds, except that, where the State provides clear and convincing evidence that all handicapped children have available to them a free appropriate public education, the Secretary may waive in part the requirement of this clause if he concurs with the evidence provided by the State;".

(2) Section 613(a) of the Act is amended by striking out "and" at the end of paragraph (11), by striking out the period at the end of paragraph (12) and inserting in lieu thereof a semicolon, and by adding at the end the following:

"(13) set forth policies and procedures for developing and implementing interagency agreements between the State educational agency and other appropriate State and local agencies to (A) define the financial responsibility of each agency for providing handicapped children and youth with free appropriate education, and (B) resolve interagency disputes, including procedures under which local educational agencies may initiate proceedings under the agreement in order to secure reimbursement from other agencies or otherwise implement the provisions of the agreement."

(3) Section 613 of the Act is amended by adding at the end the following:

"(e) This Act shall not be construed to permit a State to reduce medical and other assistance available or to alter eligibility under titles V and XIX of the Social Security Act with respect to the provision of a free appropriate public education for handicapped children within the State; and". *(42 USC 701)*

TITLE III—DISCRETIONARY PROGRAMS

SEC. 301. REGIONAL RESOURCE CENTERS.

Section 621 of the ACT (20 U.S.C. 1421) is amended to read as follows:

"REGIONAL RESOURCE AND FEDERAL CENTERS

"SEC. 621. (a) The Secretary may make grants to, or enter into contracts or cooperative agreements with, institutions of higher education, public agencies, private nonprofit organizations, State educational agencies, or combinations of such agencies or institutions (which combinations may include one or more local educational agencies) within particular regions of the United States, to pay all or part of the cost of the establishment and operation of regional resource centers. Each regional resource center shall provide consultation, technical assistance, and training to State educational agencies and through such State educational agencies to local educational agencies and to other appropriate State agencies providing early intervention services. The services provided by a regional resource center shall be consistent with the priority needs identified by the States served by the center and the findings of the Secretary in monitoring reports prepared by the Secretary under section 617 of the Act. Each regional resource center established or operated under this section shall— *(20 USC 1417)*

"(1) assist in identifying and solving persistent problems in providing quality special education and related services for handicapped children and early intervention services to handicapped infants and toddlers and their families,

"(2) assist in developing, identifying, and replicating successful programs and practices which will improve special education and related services to handicapped children and youth and their families and early intervention services to handicapped infants and toddlers and their families,

"(3) gather and disseminate information to all State educational agencies within the region and coordinate activities with other centers assisted under this subsection and other relevant projects conducted by the Department of Education,

"(4) assist in the improvement of information dissemination to and training activities for professionals and parents of handicapped infants, toddlers, children, and youth, and

"(5) provide information to and training for agencies, institutions, and organizations, regarding techniques and approaches for submitting applications for grants, contracts, and cooperative agreements under this part and parts D through G.

"(b) In determining whether to approve an application for a project under subsection (a), the Secretary shall consider the need for such a center in the region to be served by the applicant and the capability of the applicant to fulfill the responsibilities under subsection (a). *(20 USC 1422-1454)*

"(c) Each regional resource center shall report a summary of materials produced or developed and the summaries reported shall be included in the annual report to Congress required under section 618. *(20 USC 1418)* "(d) The Secretary may establish one coordinating technical assistance center focusing on national priorities established by the Secretary to assist the regional resource centers in the delivery of technical assistance, consistent with such national priorities.

"(e) Before using funds made available in any fiscal year to carry out this section for purposes of subsection (d), not less than the amount made available for this section in the previous fiscal year shall be made available for regional resource centers under subsection (a) and in no case shall more than $500,000 be made available for the center under subsection (d)."

SEC. 302. SERVICES FOR DEAF-BLIND CHILDREN AND YOUTH.

Section 622 is amended by adding at the end thereof the following new subsections: *(20 USC 1422)*

"(e) The Secretary is authorized to make grants to, or enter into contracts or cooperative agreements with, public or nonprofit private agencies, institutions, or organizations for the development and operation of extended school year demonstration programs for severely handicapped children and youth, including deaf-blind children and youth.

"(f) The Secretary may make grants to, or enter into contracts or cooperative agreements with, the entities under section 624(a) for the purposes in such section."

SEC. 303. EARLY EDUCATION FOR HANDICAPPED CHILDREN

Section 623 of the Act (20 U.S.C. 1423) is amended to read as follows:

"EARLY EDUCATION FOR HANDICAPPED CHILDREN

"SEC. 623. (a)(1) The Secretary may arrange by contract, grant, or cooperative agreement with appropriate public agencies and private nonprofit organizations, for the development and operation of experimental, demonstration, and outreach preschool and early intervention programs for handicapped children which the Secretary determines show promise of promoting a comprehensive and strengthened approach to the special problems of such children. Such programs shall include activities and services designed to (1) facilitate the intellectual, emotional, physical, mental, social, speech, language development, and self-help skills of such children, (2) encourage the participation of the parents of such children in the development and operation of any such program, and (3) acquaint the community to be served by any such program with the problems and potentialities of such children, (4) offer training about exemplary models and practices to State and local personnel who provide services to handicapped children from birth through eight, and (5) support the adaption of exemplary models and practices in States and local communities.

"(2) Programs authorized by paragraph (1) shall be coordinated with similar programs in the schools operated or supported by State or local educational agencies of the community to be served and with similar programs operated by other public agencies in such community.

"(3) As much as is feasible, programs assisted under paragraph (1) shall be geographically dispersed throughout the Nation in urban as well as rural areas.

"(4)(A) Except as provided in subparagraph (B), no arrangement under paragraph (1) shall provide for the payment of more than 90 percent of the total annual costs of development, operation, and evaluation of any program. Non-Federal contributions may be in cash or in kind, fairly evaluated, including plant, equipment, and services.

"(B) The Secretary may waive the requirement of subparagraph (A) in the case of an arrangement entered into under paragraph (1) with governing bodies of Indian tribes located on Federal or State reservations and with consortia of such bodies.

"(b) The Secretary shall arrange by contract, grant, or cooperative agreement with appropriate public agencies and private nonprofit organizations for the establishment of a technical assistance development system to assist entities operating experimental, demonstration, and outreach programs and to assist State agencies to expand and improve services provided to handicapped children.

"(c) The Secretary shall arrange by contract, grant, or cooperative agreement with appropriate public agencies and public nonprofit organizations for the establishment of early childhood research institutes to carry on sustained research to generate and disseminate new information on preschool and early intervention for handicapped children and their families.

"(d) The Secretary may make grants to, enter into contracts or cooperative agreements under this section with, such organizations or institutions, as are determined by the Secretary to be appropriate, for research to identify and meet the full range of special needs of handicapped children and for training of personnel for programs specifically designed for handicapped children.

"(e) At least one year before the termination of a grant, contract, or cooperative agreement made or entered into under subsections (b) and (c), the Secretary shall publish in the Federal Register a notice of intent to accept application for such a grant, contract, or cooperative agreement contingent on the appropriation of sufficient funds by Congress.

"(f) For purposes of this section the term 'handicapped children' includes children from birth through eight years of age."

SEC. 304. PROGRAMS FOR SEVERELY HANDICAPPED CHILDREN.

Section 624 of the Act (20 U.S.C. 1424) is amended to read as follows:

"PROGRAMS FOR SEVERELY HANDICAPPED CHILDREN

"SEC. 624. (a) The Secretary may make grants to, or enter into contracts or cooperative agreements with, such organizations or institutions, as are determined by the Secretary to be appropriate, to address the needs of severely handicapped children and youth, for—
"(1) research to identify and meet the full range of special needs of such handicapped children and youth,
"(2) the development or demonstration of new, or improvements in, existing, methods, approaches, or techniques which would contribute to the adjustment and education of such handicapped children and youth,
"(3) training of personnel for programs specifically designed for such children, and
"(4) dissemination of materials and information about practices found effective in working with such children and youth.
"(b) In making grants and contracts under subsection (a), the Secretary shall ensure that the activities funded under such grants and contracts will be coordinated with similar activities funded from grants and contracts under other sections of this Act.
"(c) To the extent feasible, programs, authorized by subsection (a) shall be geographically dispersed throughout the nation in urban and rural areas."

SEC. 305. POSTSECONDARY EDUCATION PROGRAMS.

Section 625 is amended to read as follows: *(20 USC 1424a)*

"POSTSECONDARY EDUCATION

"SEC. 625. (a)(1) The Secretary may make grants to, or enter into contracts with, State educational agencies, institutions of higher education, junior and community colleges, vocational and technical institutions, and other appropriate nonprofit educational agencies for the development, operation, and dissemination of specifically designed model programs of postsecondary, vocational, technical, continuing, or adult education for handicapped individuals.
"(2) In making grants or contracts on a competitive basis under paragraph (1), the Secretary shall give priority consideration to 4 regional centers for the deaf and to model programs for individuals with handicapping conditions other than deafness—
"(A) for developing and adapting programs of postsecondary, vocational, technical, continuing, or adult education to meet

the special needs of handicapped individuals, and
"(B) for programs that coordinate, facilitate, and encourage education of handicapped individuals with their nonhandicapped peers.

"(3) Persons operating programs for handicapped persons under a grant or contract under paragraph (1) must coordinate their efforts with and disseminate information about their activities to the clearinghouse on postsecondary programs established under section 633(b).

"(4) At least one year before the termination of a grant or contract with any of the 4 regional centers for the deaf, the Secretary shall publish in the Federal Register a notice of intent to accept application for such grant or contract, contingent on the appropriation of sufficient funds by Congress. *(20 USC 1433)*

"(5) To the extent feasible, programs authorized by paragraph (1) shall be geographically dispensed throughout the nation in urban and rural areas.

"(6) Of the sums made available for programs under paragraph (1), not less than $2,000,000 shall first be available for the 4 regional centers for the deaf.

"(b) For the purposes of subsection (a) the term 'handicapped individuals' means individuals who are mentally retarded, hard of hearing, deaf, speech or language impaired, visually handicapped, seriously emotionally disturbed, orthopedically impaired, other health impaired individuals, or individuals with specific learning disabilities who by reason thereof require special education and related services."

SEC. 306. SECONDARY EDUCATION AND TRANSITIONAL SERVICES FOR HANDICAPPED YOUTH.

Section 626 of the Act is amended to read as follows: *(20 USC 1425)*

"SECONDARY EDUCATION AND TRANSITIONAL SERVICES FOR HANDICAPPED YOUTH

"SEC. 626. (a) The Secretary may make grants to, or enter into contracts with, institutions of higher education, State educational agencies, local educational agencies, or other appropriate public and private nonprofit institutions or agencies (including the State job training coordinating councils and service delivery area administrative entities established under the Job Training Partnership Act (Public Law 97-300)) to— *(29 USC 1501 note)*

"(1) strengthen and coordinate special education and related services for handicapped youth currently in school or who recently left school to assist them in the transition of postsecondary education, vocational training, competitive employment (including supported employment), continuing education, or adult services,

"(2) stimulate the improvements and development of programs for secondary special education, and

"(3) stimulate the improvement of the vocational and life skills of handicapped students to enable them to be better prepared for transition to adult life and services.

To the extent feasible, such programs shall be geographically dispersed through the Nation in urban and rural areas.

"(b) Projects assisted under subsection (a) may include—

"(1) developing strategies and techniques for transition to independent living, vocational training, vocational rehabilitation, postsecondary education, and competitive employment (including supported employment) for handicapped youth,

"(2) establishing demonstration models for services, programs, and individualized education programs, which emphasize vocational training, transitional services, and placement for handicapped youth,

"(3) conducting demographic studies which provide information on the numbers, age levels, types of handicapping conditions, and services required for handicapped youth in need of transitional programs,

"(4) specially designed vocational programs to increase the potential for competitive employment for handicapped youth,

"(5) research and development projects for exemplary service delivery models and the replication and dissemination of successful models,

"(6) initiating cooperative models between educational agencies and adult service agencies, including vocational rehabilitation, mental health, mental retardation, public employment, and employers, which facilitate the planning and developing of transitional services for handicapped youth to postsecondary education and vocational training, employment, continuing education, and adult services,

"(7) developing appropriate procedures for evaluating vocational training, placement, and transitional services for handicapped youth,

"(8) conducting studies which provide information on the numbers, age levels, types of handicapping conditions and reasons why handicapped youth drop out of school,

"(9) developing special education curriculum and instructional techniques that will improve handicapped students' acquisition of the skills necessary for transition to adult life and services, and

"(10) specifically designed physical education and therapeutic recreation programs to increase the potential of handicapped youths for community participation.

(c) For purposes of paragraphs (1) and (2) of subsection (b), if an applicant is not an educational agency, such applicant shall coordinate with the State educational agency.

"(d) Applications for assistance under subsection (a) other than for the purpose of conducting studies or evaluations shall—
"(1) describe the procedures to be used for disseminating relevant findings and data to regional resource centers, clearinghouses, and other interested persons, agencies, or organizations,
"(2) describe the procedures that will be used for coordinating services among agencies for which handicapped youth are or will be eligible, and
"(3) to the extent appropriate, provide for the direct participation of handicapped students and the parents of handicapped students in the planning, development, and implementation of such projects.
"(e) The Secretary is authorized to make grants to, or to enter into contracts or cooperative agreements with, such organizations or institutions as are determined by the Secretary to be appropriate for the development or demonstration of new or improvements in existing methods, approaches, or techniques which will contribute to the adjustment and education of handicapped children and youth and the dissemination of materials and information concerning practices found effective in working with such children and youth.
"(f) The Secretary, as appropriate, shall coordinate programs described under subsection (a) with projects developed under section 311 of the Rehabilitation Act of 1973." *(29 USC 777a)*

SEC. 307. AUTHORIZATION.

Section 628 is amended to read as follows: *(20 USC 1427)*

"AUTHORIZATION OF APPROPRIATIONS

"SEC. 628. (a) There are authorized to be appropriated to carry out section 621, $6,700,000 for fiscal year 1987, $7,100,000 for fiscal year 1988, and $7,500,000 for fiscal year 1989.
"(b) There are authorized to be appropriated to carry out section 622, $15,900,000 for fiscal year 1987, $16,800,000 for fiscal year 1988, and $17,800,000 for fiscal year 1989.
"(c) There are authorized to be appropriated to carry out section 623, $24,470,000 for fiscal year 1987, $25,870,000 for fiscal year 1988, and $27,410,000 for fiscal year 1989.
"(d) There are authorized to be appropriated to carry out section 624, $5,300,000 for fiscal year 1987, $5,600,000 for fiscal year 1988, and $5,900,000 for fiscal year 1989.
"(e) There are authorized to be appropriated to carry out section 625, $5,900,000 for fiscal year 1987, $6,200,000 for fiscal year 1988, and $6,600,000 for fiscal year 1989.
"(f) There are authorized to be appropriated to carry out section 626, $7,300,000 for fiscal year 1987, $7,700,000 for fiscal year 1988, and $8,100,000 for fiscal year 1989.".

SEC. 308. GRANTS FOR PERSONNEL TRAINING.

Section 631 of the Act (20 U.S.C. 1431) is amended to read as follows:

"GRANTS FOR PERSONNEL TRAINING

"SEC. 631. (a)(1) The Secretary may make grants, which may include scholarships with necessary stipends and allowances, to institutions of higher education (including the university-affiliated facilities program under the Rehabilitation Act of 1973 and satellite network of the developmental disabilities program) and other appropriate nonprofit agencies to assist them in training personnel for careers in special education and early intervention, including—
(29 USC 701 note)
"(A) special education teaching, including speech-language pathology and audiology, and adaptive physical education,
"(B) related services to handicapped children and youth in educational settings,
"(C) special education supervision and administration,
"(D) special education research, and
"(E) training of special education personnel and other personnel providing special services and pre-school and early intervention services for handicapped children.
"(2)(A) In making grants under paragraph (1), the Secretary shall base the determination of such grants on information relating to the present and projected need for the personnel to be trained based on identified State, regional, or national shortages, and the capacity of the institution or agency to train qualified personnel, and other information considered appropriate by the Secretary.
"(B) The Secretary shall ensure that grants are only made under paragraph (1) to applicant agencies and institutions that meet State and professionally recognized standards for the preparation of special education and related services personnel unless the grant is for the purpose of assisting the applicant agency or institution to meet such standards.
"(3) Grants under paragraph (1) may be used by institutions to assist in covering the cost of courses of training or study for such personnel and for establishing and maintaining fellowships or traineeships with such stipends and allowances as may be determined by the Secretary.
"(4) The Secretary in carrying out paragraph (1) may reserve a sum not to exceed 5 percent of the amount available for paragraph (1) in each fiscal year for contracts to prepare personnel in areas where shortages exist when a response to that need has not been adequately addressed by the grant process.
"(b) The Secretary may make grants to institutions of higher education and other appropriate nonprofit agencies to conduct special

projects to develop and demonstrate new approaches (including the application of new technology) for the preservice training purposes set forth in subsection (a), for regular educators, for the training of teachers to work in community and school settings with handicapped secondary school students, and for the inservice training of special education personnel, including classroom aides, related services personnel, and regular education personnel who serve handicapped children and personnel providing early intervention services.

"(c)(1) The Secretary may make grants through a separate competition to private nonprofit organizations for the purpose of providing training and information to parents of handicapped children and persons who work with parents to enable such individuals to participate more effectively with professionals in meeting the educational needs of handicapped children. Such grants shall be designed to meet the unique training and information needs of parents of handicapped children living in the area to be served by the grant, particularly those who are members of groups that have been traditionally underrepresented.

"(2) In order to receive a grant under paragraph (1) a private nonprofit organization shall—

"(A) be governed by a board of directors on which a majority of the members are parents of handicapped children and which includes members who are professionals in the field of special education and related services who serve handicapped children and youth, or if the nonprofit private organization does not have such a board, such organization shall have a membership which represents the interests of individuals with handicapping conditions, and shall establish a special governing committee on which a majority of the members are parents of handicapped children and which includes members who are professionals in the fields of special education and related services to operate the training and information program under paragraph (1).

"(B) serve the parents of children with the full range of handicapping conditions under such grant program, and

"(C) demonstrate the capacity and expertise to conduct effectively the training and information activities for which a grant may be made under paragraph (1).

"(3) The board of directors or special governing committee of a private nonprofit organization receiving a grant under paragraph (1) shall meet at least once in each calendar quarter to review the parent training and information activities for which the grant is made, and each such committee shall advise the governing board directly of its views and recommendations. Whenever a private nonprofit organization requests the renewal of a grant under paragraph (1) for a fiscal year, the board of directors or the special governing committee shall submit to the Secretary a written review of the parent training and information program conducted by that private nonprofit organization during the preceding fiscal year.

"(4) The Secretary shall ensure that grants under paragraph (1) will—

"(A) be distributed geographically to the greatest extent possible throughout all the States and give priority to grants which involve unserved areas, and

"(B) be targeted to parents of handicapped children in both urban and rural areas or on a State or regional basis.

"(5) Parent training and information programs assisted under paragraph (1) shall assist parents to—

"(A) better understand the nature and needs of the handicapping conditions of children,

"(B) provide followup support for handicapped children's educational programs,

"(C) communicate more effectively with special and regular educators, administrators, related services personnel, and other relevant professionals,

"(D) participate in educational decisionmaking processes including the development of a handicapped child's individualized educational program,

"(E) obtain information about the programs, services, and resources available to handicapped children and the degree to which the programs, services, and resources are appropriate, and

"(F) understand the provisions for the education of handicapped children as specified under part B of this Act. *(20 USC 1411)*

"(6) Parent training and information programs may, at a grant recipient's discretion, include State or local educational personnel where such participation will further an objective of the program assisted by the grant.

"(7) Each private nonprofit organization operating a program receiving a grant under paragraph (1) shall consult with appropriate agencies which serve or assist handicapped children and youth and are located in the jurisdictions served by the program.

"(8) The Secretary shall provide technical assistance, by grant or contract, for establishing, developing, and coordinating parent training and information programs."

SEC. 309. GRANTS FOR STATE EDUCATIONAL AGENCIES AND INSTITUTIONS FOR TRAINEESHIPS.

Section 632 of the Act (20 U.S.C. 1432) is amended to read as follows:

"GRANTS TO STATE EDUCATIONAL AGENCIES AND INSTITUTIONS FOR TRAINEESHIPS

"SEC. 632. The Secretary shall make grants to each State educational agency and may make grants to institutions of higher education to assist in establishing and maintaining preservice and inservice programs to prepare personnel to meet the needs of handicapped infants, toddlers, children, and youth or supervisors of such persons, consistent with the personnel needs identified in the State's comprehensive system of personnel development under section 613."

SEC. 310. CLEARINGHOUSES.

(a) IN GENERAL.—Subsection (a) of section 633 of the Act (20 U.S.C. 1433) is amended by striking out "to achieve" and all that follows in that subsection and inserting in lieu thereof the following: "to disseminate information and provide technical assistance on a national basis to parents, professionals, and other interested parties concerning—

"(1) programs relating to the education of the handicapped under this Act and under other Federal laws, and

"(2) participation in such programs, including referral of individuals to appropriate national, State, and local agencies and organizations for further assistance."

(b) ADDITIONAL CLEARINGHOUSE.—Section 633 of the Act is amended by redesignating subsection (c) as subsection (d) and by inserting after subsection (b) the following:

"(c) The Secretary shall make a grant or enter into a contract for a national clearinghouse designed to encourage students to seek careers and professional personnel to seek employment in the various fields relating to the education of handicapped children and youth through the following:

"(1) Collection and dissemination of information on current and future national, regional, and State needs for special education and related services personnel.

"(2) Dissemination to high school counselors and others concerning current career opportunities in special education, location of programs, and various forms of financial assistance (such as scholarships, stipends, and allowances).

"(3) Identification of training programs available around the country.

"(4) Establishment of a network among local and State educational agencies and institutions of higher education concerning the supply of graduates and available openings.

"(5) Technical assistance to institutions seeking to meet State and professionally recognized standards."

(c) TECHNICAL AMENDMENT.—The heading for section 633 of the Act is amended to read as follows:

"CLEARINGHOUSE."

SEC. 311. AUTHORIZATION.

Section 635 of the Act (20 U.S.C. 1435) is amended to read as follows:

"AUTHORIZATION OF APPROPRIATIONS

"SEC. 635. (a) There are authorized to be appropriated to carry out this part (other than section 633) $70,400,000 for fiscal year 1987, $74,500,000 for fiscal year 1988, and $79,000,000 for fiscal year 1989. There are authorized to be appropriated to carry out section 633, $1,200,000 for fiscal year 1987, $1,900,000 for fiscal year 1988, and $2,000,000 for fiscal year 1989.

"(b) Of the funds appropriated pursuant to subsection (a) for any fiscal year, the Secretary shall reserve not less than 65 per centum for activities described in subparagraphs (A) through (E) of section 631(a)(1).

"(c) Of the funds appropriated under subsection (a) for any fiscal year, the Secretary shall reserve 10 percent for activities under section 631(c).".

SEC. 312. RESEARCH AND DEMONSTRATION PROJECTS IN EDUCATION OF HANDICAPPED CHILDREN.

Section 641 of the Act (20 U.S.C. 1441) is amended to read as follows:

"RESEARCH AND DEMONSTRATION PROJECTS IN EDUCATION OF HANDICAPPED CHILDREN

"SEC. 641. (a) The Secretary may make grants to, or enter into contracts or cooperative agreements with, State and local educational agencies, institutions of higher education, and other public agencies and nonprofit private organizations for research and related activities to assist special education personnel, related services personnel, early intervention personnel, and other appropriate persons, including parents, in improving the special education and related services and early intervention services for handicapped infants, toddlers, children, and youth. Research and related activities shall be designed to increase knowledge and understanding of handicapping conditions, and teaching, learning, and education-related developmental practices and services for handicapped infants, toddlers, children and youth. Research and related activities assisted under this section shall include the following:

"(1) The development of new and improved techniques and devices for teaching handicapped infants, toddlers, children and youth.

"(2) The development of curricula which meet the unique educational and developmental needs for handicapped infants, toddlers, children and youth.

"(3) The application of new technologies and knowledge for the purpose of improving the instruction of handicapped infants, toddlers, children and youth.

"(4) The development of program models and exemplary practices areas of special education and early intervention.

"(5) The dissemination of information on research and related activities conducted under this part to regional resource centers and interested individuals and organizations.

"(6) The development of instruments, including tests, inventories, and scales for measuring progress of handicapped infants, toddlers, children and youth across a number of developmental domains.

"(b) In carrying out subsection (a), the Secretary shall consider the special education or early intervention experience of applicants under such subsection.

"(c) The Secretary shall publish proposed research priorities in the Federal Register every 2 years, not later than July 1, and shall allow a period of 60 days for public comments and suggestions. After analyzing and considering the public comments, the Secretary shall publish final research priorities in the Federal Register not later than 30 days after the close of the comment period.

"(d) The Secretary shall provide an index (including the title of each research project and the name and address of the researching organization) of all research projects conducted in the prior fiscal year in the annual report described under section 618. The Secretary shall make reports of research projects available to the education community at large and to other interested parties.

"(e) The Secretary shall coordinate the research priorities established under subsection (c) with research priorities established by the National Institute of Handicapped Research and shall provide information concerning research priorities established under such subsection to the National Council on the Handicapped, and to the Bureau of Indian Affairs Advisory Committee for Exceptional Children."

SEC. 313. PANELS AND EXPERTS.

Section 643 of the Act (20 U.S.C. 1443) is amended to read as follows:

"PANELS OF EXPERTS

"SEC. 643. (a) The Secretary shall convene, in accordance with subsection (b), panels of experts who are competent to evaluate proposals for projects under parts C through G. The panels shall be composed of — *(20 USC 1421-1454)*

"(1) individuals from the field of special education for the handicapped and other relevant disciplines who have significant expertise and experience in the content areas and age levels addressed in the proposals, and

"(2) handicapped individuals and parents of handicapped individuals when appropriate.

"(b)(1) The Secretary shall convene panels under subsection (a) for any application which includes a total funding request exceeding $60,000 and may convene or otherwise appoint panels for applications which include funding requests that are less than such amount.

"(2) Such panels shall include a majority of non-Federal members. Such non-Federal members shall be provided travel and per diem not to exceed the rate provided to other educational consultants used by the Department and shall be provided consultant fees at such a rate.

"(c) The Secretary may use funds available under parts C through G to pay expenses and fees of non-Federal members under subsection (b)." *(20 USC 1421-1454)*

SEC. 314. AUTHORIZATION.

Section 644 of the Act (20 U.S.C. 1444) is amended to read as follows:

"AUTHORIZATION OF APPROPRIATIONS

"SEC. 644. For purposes of carrying out this part, there are authorized to be appropriated $18,000,000 for fiscal year 1987, $19,000,000 for fiscal year 1988, and $20,100,000 for fiscal year 1989.".

SEC. 315. CAPTIONED FILMS AND EDUCATIONAL MEDIA FOR HANDICAPPED PERSONS.

(a) ILLITERACY. — Subsection (a) of section 652 of the Act (20 U.S.C. 1452) is amended —
  (1) by striking out "in accordance with regulations" and inserting in lieu thereof ", including for the purpose of addressing problems of illiteracy among the handicapped",
  (2) by inserting after "available" the following: ", in accordance with regulations,".

(b) AUTHORIZED USES. — (1) Subsection (b)(4) of section 652 of the Act is amended by inserting after "handicapped" the following: ", public libraries,".

(2) Subsection (b)(7) is amended by striking the period and inserting in lieu thereof "; and", and by adding the following:

"(8) provide by grant or contract for educational media and materials for the deaf."

(c) NATIONAL THEATRE OF THE DEAF. — Section 652 of the Act is amended by adding at the end the following:

"(c) The Secretary may make grants to or enter into contracts or cooperative agreements with the National Theatre of the Deaf, Inc. for the purpose of providing theatrical experiences to—
 "(1) enrich the lives of deaf children and adults,
 "(2) increase public awareness and understanding of deafness and the artistic and intellectual achievements of deaf people, and
 "(3) promote the integration of hearing and deaf people through shared cultural experiences."

SEC. 316. AUTHORIZATION.

Section 653 of the Act (20 U.S.C. 1453) is repealed and section 654 of the Act (20 U.S.C. 1454) is redesignated as section 653 and amended to read as follows:

"AUTHORIZATION

"SEC. 653. For the purposes of carrying out this part, there are authorized to be appropriated $15,000,000 for fiscal year 1987, $15,750,000 for fiscal year 1988, and $16,540,000 for fiscal year 1989." *(20 USC 1454)*

SEC. 317. TECHNOLOGY, EDUCATIONAL MEDIA, AND MATERIALS FOR THE HANDICAPPED.

The Act is amended by adding after part F the following: *(20 USC 1451)*

"PART G — TECHNOLOGY, EDUCATIONAL MEDIA AND MATERIALS FOR THE HANDICAPPED

"FINANCIAL ASSISTANCE

SEC. 661. The Secretary may make grants or enter into contracts or cooperative agreements with institutions of higher education, State and local educational agencies, or other appropriate agencies and organizations for the purpose of advancing the use of new technology, media, and materials in the education of handicapped students and the provision of early intervention to handicapped infants and toddlers. In carrying out this subsection, the Secretary may fund projects or centers for the purposes of — *(20 USC 1461)*
 "(1) determining how technology, media, and materials are being used in the education of the handicapped and how they can be used more effectively,
 "(2) designing and adapting new technology, media, and materials to improve the education of handicapped students,
 "(3) assisting the public and private sectors in the development

and marketing of new technology, media, and materials for the education of the handicapped, and

"(4) disseminating information on the availability and use of new technology, media, and materials for the education of the handicapped.

"AUTHORIZATION OF APPROPRIATIONS

"SEC. 662. For the purposes of carrying out this part, there are authorized to be appropriated $10,000,000 for fiscal year 1987, $10,500,000 for fiscal year 1988, and $11,025,000 for fiscal year 1989." *(20 USC 1462)*

TITLE IV — MISCELLANEOUS

SEC. 401. REMOVAL OF ARCHITECTURAL BARRIERS.

Section 607(a) of the Act (20 U.S.C. 1406) is amended by inserting "with the Secretary of the Interior and" after "cooperative agreements".

SEC. 402. DEFINITIONS.

Section 602(a) of the Act (20 U.S.C. 1401(a)) is amended —
   (1) in paragraph (11), by striking out "and" at the end of subparagraph (D), by striking out the period at the end of subparagraph (E) and inserting in lieu thereof " and", and by adding at the end the following:
      "(F) The term includes community colleges receiving funding from the Secretary of the Interior under Public Law 95-471.", and *(25 USC 1801 note)*
   (2) by adding at the end the following:
"(23)(A) The term 'public or private nonprofit agency or organization' includes an Indian tribe.
"(B) The terms 'Indian', 'American Indian', and 'Indian American' mean an individual who is a member of an Indian tribe.
"(C) The term 'Indian tribe' means any Federal or State Indian tribe, band, rancheria, pueblo, colony, or community, including any Alaskan native village or regional village corporation (as defined in or established under the Alaska Native Claims Settlement Act)." *(43 USC 1601 note)*

SEC. 403. ALLOCATION: STATE ADMINISTRATION

   (a) ALLOCATION. — Section 611(a)(5)(A) of the Act (20 U.S.C. 1411(a)(5)(A) is amended to read as follows:
"(5)(A) In determining the allotment of each State under paragraph (1), the Secretary may not count —

"(i) handicapped children aged three to seventeen, inclusive, in such State under paragraph (1)(A) to the extent the number of such children is greater than 12 percent of the number of all children aged three to seventeen, inclusive, in such State and the State serves all handicapped children aged three to five, inclusive, in the State pursuant to State law or practice or the order of any court,

"(ii) handicapped children aged five to seventeen, inclusive, in such State under paragraph (1)(A) to the extent the number of such children is greater than 12 percent of the number of all children aged five to seventeen, inclusive, in such State and the States does not serve all handicapped children aged three to five inclusive, in the State pursuant to State law or practice on the order of any court; and

"(iii) handicapped children who are counted under section 121 of the Elementary and Secondary Education Act of 1965." *(20 USC 2731)*

(b) STATE ADMINISTRATION. — Section 611(c)(2)(A)(ii) of the Act (20 U.S.C. 1411(c)(2)(A)(ii)) is amended to read as follows:

"(ii) the part remaining after use in accordance with clause (i) shall be used by the State (I) to provide support services and direct services in accordance with the priorities established under section 612(3), and (II) for the administrative costs of monitoring and complaint investigation but only to the extent that such costs exceed the costs of administration incurred during fiscal year 1985." *(20 USC 1412)*

SEC. 404. INDIANS.

Subsection (f) of section 611 of such Act (20 U.S.C. 1411) is amended to read as follows:

"(f)(1) The Secretary shall make payments to the Secretary of the Interior according to the need for assistance for the education of handicapped children on reservations serviced by elementary and secondary schools operated for Indian children by the Department of the Interior. The amount of such payment for any fiscal year shall be 1.25 percent of the aggregate amounts available to all States under this section for that fiscal year.

"(2) The Secretary of the Interior may receive an allotment under paragraph (1) only after submitting to the Secretary an application which —

"(A) meets the applicable requirements of sections 612, 613, and 614(a), *(20 USC 1412)*

"(B) includes satisfactory assurance that all handicapped children aged 3 to 5, inclusive receive a free appropriate public education by or before the 1987-1988 school year, *(20 USC 1414)*

"(C) includes an assurance that there are public hearings, adequate notice of such hearings, and an opportunity for comment afforded to members of tribes, tribal governing bodies, and designated local school boards before adoption of the policies, programs, and procedures required under sections 612, 613, and 614(a), and

"(D) is approved by the Secretary.

Section 616 shall appy to any such application." *(20 USC 1416)*

SEC. 405. QUALIFIED PERSONNEL

Section 613(a) of the Act (20 U.S.C. 1413) is amended by inserting at the end thereof the following:

"(14) policies and procedures relating to the establishment and maintenance of standards to ensure that personnel necessary to carry out the purposes of this part are appropriately and adequately prepared and trained, including—

"(A) the establishment and maintenance of standards which are consistent with any State approved or recognized certification, licensing, registration, or other comparable requirements which apply to the area in which he or she is providing special education or related services, and

"(B) to the extent such standards are not based on the highest requirements in the State applicable to a specific profession or discipline, the steps the State is taking to require the retraining or hiring of personnel that meet appropriate professional requirements in the State."

SEC. 406. EVALUATION.

Section 618 of the Act (20 U.S.C. 1418) is amended to read as follows:

"EVALUATION

"SEC. 618. (a) The Secretary shall directly or by grant, contract, or cooperative agreement, collect data and conduct studies, investigations, and evaluations—

"(1) to assess progress in the implementation of this Act, the impact, and the effectiveness of State and local efforts and efforts by the Secretary of Interior to provide free appropriate public education to all handicapped children and youth and early intervention services to handicapped infants and toddlers, and

"(2) to provide—

"(A) Congress with information relevant to policymaking, and

"(B) Federal, State, and local agencies and the Secretary of Interior with information relevant to program management, administration, and effectiveness with respect to such education and early intervention services.

"(b) In carrying out subsection (a), the Secretary, on at least an annual basis, shall obtain data concerning programs and projects assisted under this Act and under other Federal laws relating to handicapped infants, toddlers, children, and youth, and such additional information, from State and local educational agencies, the Secretary of Interior, and other appropriate sources, as is necessary for the implementation of this Act including—

"(1) the number of handicapped infants, toddlers, children, and youth in each State receiving a free appropriate public education or early intervention services (A) in age groups 0-2 and 3-5, and (B) in age groups 6-11, 12-17, and 18-21 by disability category,

"(2) the number of handicapped children and youth in each State who are participating in regular educational programs (consistent with the requirements of sections 612(5)(B) and 614(a)(1)(C)(iv) by disability category, and the number of handicapped children and youth in separate classes, separate schools or facilities, or public or private residential facilities or who have been otherwise removed from the regular education environment, *(20 USC 1412, 1414)*

"(3) the number of handicapped children and youth exiting the educational system each year through program completion or otherwise (A) in age group 3-5, and (B) in age groups 6-11, 12-17, and 18-21 by disability category and anticipated services for the next year,

"(4) the amount of Federal, State, and local funds expended in each State specifically for special education and related services and for early intervention services (which may be based upon a sampling of data from State agencies including State and local educational agencies),

"(5) the number and type of personnel that are employed in the provision of special education and related services to handicapped children and youth and early intervention services to handicapped infants and toddlers by disability category served, and the estimated number and type of additional personnel by disability category needed to adequately carry out the policy established by this Act, and

"(6) a descrption of the special education and related services and early intervention services needed to fully implement this Act throughout each State, including estimates of the number of handicapped infants and toddlers in the 0-2 age group and estimates of the number of handicapped children and youth (A) in age group 3-5 and (B) in age groups 6-11, 12-17, and 18-21 and by disability category.

"(c) The Secretary shall, by grant, contract, or cooperative agreement, provide for evaluation studies to determine the impact of this Act. Each such evaluation shall include recommendations for improvement of the programs under this Act. The Secretary shall, not later than July 1 of each year, submit to the appropriate committees of each House of the Congress and publish in the Federal Register proposed evaluation priorities for review and comment.

"(d)(1) The Secretary may enter into cooperative agreements with State educational agencies and other State agencies to carry out studies to assess the impact and effectiveness of programs assisted under this Act.

"(2) An agreement under paragraph (1) shall—

"(A) provide for the payment of not to exceed 60 percent of the total cost of studies conducted by a participating State agency to assess the impact and effectiveness of programs assisted under this Act, and

"(B) be developed in consultation with the State Advisory Panel established under this Act, the local educational agencies, and others involved in or concerned with the education of handicapped children and youth and the provision of early intervention services to handicapped infants and toddlers.

"(3) The Secretary shall provide technical assistance to participating State agencies in the implementation of the study design, analysis, and reporting procedures.

"(4) In addition, the Secretary shall disseminate information from such studies to State agencies, regional resources centers, and clearinghouses established by this Act, and, as appropriate, to others involved in, or concerned with, the education of handicapped children and youth and the provision of early intervention services to handicapped infants and toddlers.

"(e)(1) At least one study shall be a longitudinal study of a sample of handicapped students, encompassing the full range of handicapping conditions, examining their educational progress while in special education and their occupational, educational and independent living status after graduating from secondary school or otherwise leaving special education.

"(2) At least one study shall focus on obtaining and compiling current information available, through State educational agencies and local educational agencies and other service providers, regarding State and local expenditures for educational services for handicapped students (including special education and related services) and shall gather information needed in order to calculate a range of per pupil expenditures by handicapping condition.

"(f)(1) Not later than 120 days after the close of each fiscal year, the Secretary shall publish and disseminate an annual report on the progress being made toward the provision of a free appropriate public education to all handicapped children and youth and early intervention services for handicapped infants and toddlers. The annual report shall be transmitted to the appropriate committees of each House of Congress and published and disseminated in sufficient quantities to the education community at large and to other interested parties.

"(2) The Secretary shall include in each annual report under paragraph (1)—
"(A) a compilation and analysis of data gathered under subsection (b)
"(B) an index and summary of each evaluation activity and results of studies conducted under subsection (c),
"(C) a description of findings and determinations resulting from monitoring reviews of State implementation of part B of this Act, *(20 USC 1411)*
"(D) an analysis and evaluation of the participation of handicapped children and youth in vocational education programs and services,
"(E) an analysis and evaluation of the effectiveness of procedures undertaken by each State educational agency, local educational agency, and intermediate educational unit to ensure that handicapped children and youth receive special education and related services in the least restrictive environment commensurate with their needs and to improve programs of instruction for handicapped children and youth in day or residential facilities, and
"(F) any recommendation for change in the provisions of this Act or any other Federal law providing support for the education of handicapped children and youth.
"(3) In the annual report under paragraph (1) for fiscal year 1985 which is published in 1986 and for every third year thereafter, the Secretary shall include in the annual report—
"(A) an index of all current projects funded under parts C through G of this title, and *(20 USC 1421-1454)*
"(B) data reported under sections 621, 622, 623, 627, 634, 641 and 661.
"(4) In the annual report under paragraph (1) for fiscal year 1988 which is published in 1989, the Secretary shall include special sections addressing the provision of a free appropriate public education to handicapped infants, toddlers, children, and youth in rural areas and to handicapped migrants, handicapped Indians (particularly programs operated under section 611(f), handicapped Native Hawaiian, and other native Pacific basin children and youth, handicapped infants, toddlers, children and youth of limited English proficiency. *(20 USC 1426, 1434)*
"(5) Beginning in 1986, in consultation with the National Council for the Handicapped and the Bureau of Indian Affairs Advisory Committee for Exceptional Children, a description of the status of early intervention services for handicapped infants and toddlers from birth through age two, inclusive, and special education and related services to handicapped children from 3 through 5 years of age (including those receiving services through Head Start, Developmental Disabilities Programs, Crippled Children's Services, Mental Health/Mental Retardation Agency, and State child-development

centers and private agencies under contract with local schools).

"(g) There are authorized to be appropriated $3,800,000 for fiscal year 1987, $4,000,000 for fiscal year 1988, and $4,200,000 for fiscal year 1989 to carry out this section."

SEC. 407. REPEAL.

Section 604 of the Act (20 U.S.C. 1403) is repealed.

Approved October 8, 1986.

Appendix B
Minimum Age Mandates

Appendix B

Minimum Ages Mandated By States And Territories For Providing Special Education To All Handicapped Children, July 1985

Birth	Age 2	Age 3	Age 4	Age 5	Age 6 or "school-age"
Iowa	Virginia	Alaska	Delaware[1]	Arizona	Alabama
Maryland		California	Minnesota	Arkansas	Florida
Michigan		Connecticut	Oklahoma[2]	Colorado	Georgia
Nebraska		District of Columbia	Tennessee	Kansas	Idaho
New Jersey		Hawaii		Maine	Indiana
Oregon		Illinois		Missouri	Kentucky
South Dakota		Louisiana		Nevada	Mississippi
American Samoa		Massachusetts		New Mexico[3]	Montana
U.S. Trust Territories		New Hampshire		New York	Vermont
Guam		North Dakota		North Carolina	Wyoming[4]
		Rhode Island		Ohio	
		Texas[6]		Pennsylvania[5]	
		Washington		South Carolina	
		Wisconsin		Utah	

Minimum Ages Mandated By States And Territories (Cont.)

Birth	Age 2	Age 3	Age 4	Age 5	Age 6 or "school-age"
		Northern Mariana Islands		West Virginia[7] Puerto Rico Virgin Islands	

[1]Mandates services for deaf, blind, deaf-blind and autistic children from birth; mandates services for orthopedically impaired, severely mentally handicapped and trainable mentally handicapped children from age 3.
[2]Mandates services for deaf-blind and "failure to thrive" children from birth.
[3]Will phase in mandated services for 3-year-old developmentally disabled children by 1988.
[4]Health and social services are mandated for children from birth.
[5]Services mandated from 4 years 7 months.
[6]Mandates services for visually impaired, hearing impaired and deaf-blind children from birth.
[7]Will phase in mandated services for severely handicapped children by 1987.

Source: U.S. Education Department

Appendix C
Estimated Allocations, Fiscal 1987

Appendix C

Estimated State Allocations For Early Intervention Services Under P.L. 99-457, Fiscal Year 1987*

State	Population Birth through Two Years	State's Percent of Total Population	Estimated Allocation (in thousands of dollars)
Alabama	180,448	1.8%	$842
Alaska	24,461	0.2	244
Arizona	131,960	1.3	615
Arkansas	106,859	1.0	498
California	1,053,593	10.3	4,914
Colorado	134,009	1.3	625
Connecticut	112,484	1.1	525
Delaware	25,000	0.2	244
District of Columbia	21,213	0.2	244
Florida	348,556	3.4	1,626
Georgia	254,122	2.5	1,185
Hawaii	48,149	0.5	244
Idaho	58,032	0.6	271
Illinois	516,554	5.0	2,409
Indiana	255,647	2.5	1,192
Iowa	137,134	1.3	640
Kansas	111,892	1.1	522
Kentucky	172,152	1.7	803
Louisiana	223,113	2.2	1,041
Maine	47,976	0.5	244
Maryland	167,225	1.6	780
Massachusetts	206,001	2.0	961
Michigan	419,949	4.1	1,959
Minnesota	191,452	1.9	893
Mississippi	131,590	1.3	614
Missouri	218,498	2.1	1,019
Montana	39,920	0.4	244
Nebraska	75,852	0.7	354
Nevada	34,825	0.3	244
New Hampshire	38,336	0.4	244
New Jersey	280,299	2.7	1,307
New Mexico	71,173	0.7	332
New York	690,587	6.7	3,221
North Carolina	245,771	2.4	1,146
North Dakota	34,163	0.3	244
Ohio	482,262	4.7	2,249
Oklahoma	142,734	1.4	666
Oregon	121,932	1.2	569
Pennsylvania	455,755	4.5	2,126

Estimated State Allocations (Cont.)

State	Population Birth through Two Years	State's Percent of Total Population	Estimated Allocation (in thousands of dollars)
Rhode Island	34,881	0.3%	$244
South Carolina	145,656	1.4	679
South Dakota	36,349	0.4	244
Tennessee	199,300	1.9	930
Texas	716,200	7.0	3,340
Utah	119,881	1.2	559
Vermont	21,977	0.2	244
Virginia	221,302	2.2	1,032
Washington	189,339	1.9	883
West Virginia	88,090	0.9	411
Wisconsin	213,809	2.1	997
Wyoming	28,103	0.3	244
Puerto Rico	206,710	2.0	964
Total	**10,233,775**	**100%**	**$48,875**

* *The estimates are based on 1980 U.S. Census data and assume all states will apply for funds to serve handicapped infants and oddlers in fiscal 1987. The U.S. Education Department, which will distribute the funds, will decide what census data to use in determining actual state allocations.*

Note: Under P.L. 99-457, 1 percent of the appropriation may be allocated to U.S. territories (not listed above) and 1.25 percent must be allocated to the U.S. Interior Department for programs for Native Americans. Therefore, the total amount remaining for allocation to the fifty states, the District of Columbia and Puerto Rico is assumed to be $48,875,000. Under the law, all states must receive a minimum of 0.5 percent, or $244,375.

Source: Congressional Research Service

Appendix D
Entry Level Skills Checklist

Appendix D

Project STEPS' Entry Level Skills Checklist

CHILD'S NAME: _____

TEACHER: _____

DATE OF BIRTH: _____

HANDICAPPING CONDITIONS: _____

PRESCHOOL: _____

SKILL	PRETEST DATE:				MID YEAR TEST DATE:				POST-TEST DATE:		
CLASSROOM RULES	YES	NO	I/E*	TARGET SKILLS	YES	NO	I/E*	TARGET SKILLS	YES	NO	I/E*
1) Walks rather than runs indoors											
2) Waits quietly in line											
3) Sits or waits appropriately											

Project STEPS' Entry Level Skills Checklist (Cont.)

SKILL	PRETEST DATE:				MID YEAR TEST DATE:					POST-TEST DATE:		
CLASSROOM RULES (Cont.)	YES	NO	I/E*	TARGET SKILLS	YES	NO	I/E*	TARGET SKILLS	YES	NO	I/E*
4) Complies with simple direction provided to a group											
5) Makes transitions from one activity to another with minimal assistance											
6) Raises hand and/or gets teacher attention when necessary											
7) Replaces material, cleans up own work place											
8) Stays in own space for activity											
9) Stays with group outside classroom											
WORK SKILLS											
1) Refrains from disturbing the activity of others											
2) Stops activity when given direction "stop"											

Project STEPS' Entry Level Skills Checklist (Cont.)

SKILL	PRETEST DATE:				MID YEAR TEST DATE:				POST-TEST DATE:		
	YES	NO	I/E*	TARGET SKILLS	YES	NO	I/E*	TARGET SKILLS	YES	NO	I/E*
WORK SKILLS (Cont.)											
3) Holds or manipulates objects/materials											
4) Works independently on developmentally appropriate material											
5) Produces work of acceptable quality given developmentally appropriae material											
6) Completes tasks given developmentally appropriate material											
7) Follows 1-2-3 part directions related to task											
8) Attends to/works on assigned task for 1-3-5-10-15 minutes											
9) Waits until directions are completed to begin task											

Project STEPS' Entry Level Skills Checklist (Cont.)

SKILL	PRETEST DATE:				MID YEAR TEST DATE:				POST-TEST DATE:		
	YES	NO	I/E*	TARGET SKILLS	YES	NO	I/E*	TARGET SKILLS	YES	NO	I/E*
COMMUNICATION SKILLS											
1) Comes to adult when signaled											
2) Communicates own needs and preferences											
3) Answers questions about self/family; name - address - age - birthdate - parents' name											
4) Attends to peer or adult who is talking to a group											
SOCIAL BEHAVIOR SKILLS											
1) Responds positively to social recognition and reinforcement											
2) Modifies behavior when provided with verbal direction											
3) Follows school rules											

Project STEPS' Entry Level Skills Checklist (Cont.)

SKILL	PRETEST DATE:				MID YEAR TEST DATE:				POST-TEST DATE:		
	YES	NO	I/E*	TARGET SKILLS	YES	NO	I/E*	TARGET SKILLS	YES	NO	I/E*
SOCIAL BEHAVIOR SKILLS (Cont.)											
4) Separates from parents and accepts school personnel											
5) Interacts cooperatively with others											
6) Respects others and their property											
7) Expresses emotions and feelings appropriately											
8) Refrains from self-abusive behaviors											
9) Refrains from physically aggressive behavior: hitting, biting											
10) Refrains from using obscene language											
11) Defends self appropriately											
12) Is willing to try something new											
13) Waits to take turns and shares											
14) Uses imitative behavior appropriately											

Project STEPS' Entry Level Skills Checklist (Cont.)

SKILL	PRETEST DATE:			MID YEAR TEST DATE:			POST-TEST DATE:	
	YES	NO	I/E*	TARGET SKILLS	YES	NO	I/E*	TARGET SKILLS	YES	NO	I/E*
SELF MANAGEMENT SKILLS									
1) Eats lunch or snack with minimal assistance									
2) Is aware of/attends to appearance, e.g., keeps nose clean, adjusts clothing									
3) Locates and uses public restroom									
4) Cares for bathroom needs									
5) Locates other areas of school and playground									
6) Puts on/takes off outer clothing with minimal assistance									
7) Makes transitions between classroom and transportation with minimal assistance									
8) Seeks out adult if hurt or cannot handle social situations									

Project STEPS' Entry Level Skills Checklist (Cont.)

SKILL	PRETEST DATE:				MID YEAR TEST DATE:				POST-TEST DATE:		
	YES	NO	I/E*	TARGET SKILLS	YES	NO	I/E*	TARGET SKILLS	YES	NO	I/E*
SELF MANAGEMENT SKILLS (Cont.)											
9) Is aware of obvious dangers and avoids them											
10) Locates own possessions and returns them to appropriate place											

*I/E - Inconsistent/Emerging

Appendix E
U.S. Office Of Special Education Programs Directory

Appendix E

Office of Special Education Programs
U.S. Education Department

The Office of Special Education Programs of the U.S. Education Department is located at 330 C St. SW, Washington, D.C. 20202. Key officials of the office can be contacted at the telephone numbers listed below.

G. Thomas Bellamy, Director
(202)732-1007

    Patricia J. Guard, Deputy Director
    (202)732-1007

    Max Mueller, Director
    Division of Assistance to States
    (202)732-1014

        Jeff Champagne, Branch Chief
        Program Administration Branch
        (202)732-1056

        Etta Waugh, Branch Chief
        Program Assistance Branch
        (202)732-1052

        Max Mueller, Acting Branch Chief
        Program Review Branch
        (202)732-1014

    Thomas Behrens, Director
    Division of Educational Services
    (202)732-1154

        Mac Norwood, Branch Chief
        Captioning and Adaptation Branch
        (202)732-1172

        Thomas Finch, Branch Chief
        Early Childhood Branch
        (202)732-1084

        William Halloran, Branch Chief
        Secondary Education and Transitional Services Branch
        (202)732-1112

Paul Thompson, Branch Chief
Severely Handicapped Branch
(202)732-1161

Martin Kaufman, Director
Division of Innovation and Development
(202)732-1106

Nancy Safer, Branch Chief
Directed Research Branch
(202)732-1109

Jim Johnson, Branch Chief
Research Development Project Branch
(202)732-1123

Lou Danielson, Acting Branch Chief
Special Studies Branch
(202)732-1119

Norman Howe, Acting Director
Division of Personnel Preparation
(202)732-1070

William Peterson, Branch Chief
Leadership Personnel Branch
(202)732-1083

Harvey Liebergott, Branch Chief
Related Personnel Branch
(202)732-1082

Edward Moore, Branch Chief
Special Education Personnel Branch
(202)732-1048

Paul Ackerman, Director
Division of Programs, Analysis and Planning
(202)732-1155

Cathy DeLuca, Acting Branch Chief
Program Operations Branch
(202)732-1093

Bill Wolf, Acting Branch Chief
Program Planning and Information Branch
(202)732-1009

Source: U.S. Education Department

Appendix F
State Resource Directory

Appendix F

State Resource Directory

ALABAMA

State Director:
Anne Ramsey
Coordinator
Student Instructional Services
State Department of Education
1020 Monticello Court
Montgomery, Ala. 36117
(205)261-5099

State Plan Grant Representative:
Sheree Litchfield
State Plan Grant Director
Alabama Department of Education
1020 Monticello Court
Montgomery, Ala. 36117
(205)261-5099

Regional Resource Center Parent Representative:
Ann James
6607 Hollis Dr.
Montgomery, Ala. 36117
(205)272-3392

Federally Funded Parent Training Grant:
Carol Blades
President
Special Education Action Committee
P.O. Box 81112
Mobile, Ala. 36689
(205)633-9588

ALASKA

State Director:
William Mulnix
Administrator
Office of Special Services
Alaska Department of Education
P.O. Box F
Juneau, Alaska 99811
(907)465-2970

State Plan Grant Representatives:
Karen Lamb
State Plan Grant Coordinator
Alaska Department of Education
1231 Gambell St.
Anchorage, Alaska 99501
(907)277-1651

Christine Niemi
State Plan Grant Program Manager
Alaska Department of Education
P.O. Box F 801, W. Tenth St.
Juneau, Alaska 99811
(907)456-2970

Regional Resource Center Parent Representatives:
Connie Ellingson
901 Lake Box 1214
Sitka, Alaska 99835
(907)747-8064

Sherrel Hodge
P.O. Box 82
Central, Alaska 99730
(907)520-5114

State Parent Group:
Marsha Buck
SE RRC
218 Front St.
Juneau, Alaska 99801
(907)586-6806

AMERICAN SAMOA

State Director:
Jane French
Director of Special Education
Department of Education
Pago Pago, American Samoa 96799
(684)633-1323

State Plan Grant Representative:
Linda Avegalio
State Plan Grant Program Director
Special Education Division
Box 434
Pago Pago, America Samoa 96799
(684)633-1323 or 633-4789

ARIZONA

State Director:
Diane Peterson
Deputy Associate Superintendent
Special Education Section
Department of Education
1535 W. Jefferson
Phoenix, Ariz. 85007
(602)255-3183

State Plan Grant Representatives:
Gene Gardner
Arizona Department of Education
1535 W. Jefferson
Phoenix, Ariz. 85202
(602)255-3182

Jo Ann Woodley
Preschool Project Specialist
Arizona Department of Education
1535 W. Jefferson
Phoenix, Ariz. 85202
(602)255-3183

Regional Resource Center Parent Representative:
Barbara Gear
6817 N. 57th Place
Paradise Valley, Ariz. 86253
(602)263-8484 or 998-0533

Federally Funded Parent Training Grant:
Mary Slaughter
Pilot Parents
121 East Voltaire Ave.
Phoenix, Ariz. 85022
(602)863-4048

ARKANSAS

State Director:
Diane Sydoriak
Associate Director of Special Education
Arkansas Department of Education
Education Bldg., Room 105-C
S4 Capitol Mall
Little Rock, Ark. 72201
(501)371-2161

State Plan Grant Representatives:
Mary Kaye Curry
State Plan Grant Project Coordinator
Arkansas Department of Education
#4 Capitol Mall, Room 105C
Little Rock, Ark. 72201
(501)371-1686

Larance Johnson
State Plan Grant Research Associate
Arkansas Department of Education
#4 Capitol Mall, Room 105-C
Little Rock, Ark. 72201
(501)371-1686

Regional Resource Center Parent Representative:
Patsy Fordyce
7 McKinley Circle
Little Rock, Ark. 72207
(501)376-3420 (o) or
(501)666-6021 (h)

Federally Funded Parent Training Grants:
Paul Kelly
Arkansas Coalition for the Handicapped
519 E. Fifth St.
Little Rock, Ark. 72202
(501)376-0378

Barbara Semrau
Focus, Inc.
2917 King St., Suite C
Little Rock, Ark. 72202
(501)935-2750

State Resource Directory

BUREAU OF INDIAN AFFAIRS

Charles Cordova
Bureau of Exceptional Education
 Chief
Office of Indian Education
 Programs
Bureau of Indian Affairs
18th and C Sts. NW, Room 4642
Washington, D.C. 20245
(202)343-4071

CALIFORNIA

State Director:
Shirley Thornton
Associate Superintendent/Director
Specialized Programs Branch
Special Education Division
P.O. Box 944272
Sacramento, Calif. 94244
(916)323-4768

State Plan Grant Representatives:
Doug McDougal
State Plan Grant Program
 Coordinator
California Department of Education
Office of Special Education
721 Capitol Mall
Sacramento, Calif. 95814
(916)323-6673

Betsy Qualls
State Plan Grant Program Director
California Department of Education
Office of Special Education
721 Capitol Mall
Sacramento, Calif. 95814
(916)323-6673

*Regional Resource Center Parent
 Representative:*
Beverly Doyle
3740 Bolsa Court
Sacramento, Calif. 95864
(916)921-0521

*Federally Funded Parent Training
 Grant:*
Joan Tellefsen
Team of Advocates for Special Kids
Task Parent Training Projects
1800 E. La Veta Ave.
Orange, Calif. 92666
(714)771-6542

State Parent Groups:
Prudy Stephens
Special Education Parent Facilitator
 Program
Whittier School
3401 Clairemont Dr., Room 7A
San Diego, Calif. 92117

COPE
Joanne Travers
UCP of California
P.O. Box 1475
Upland, Calif. 91785

Parents Helping Parents, Inc.
Florence Payadue
535 Race St., Suite 220
San Jose, Calif. 95126
(408)288-5010

Jean Styris
Special Education Community
 Advisory Committee Network
1610 Franrose Lane
Concord, Calif. 94519
(415)827-3863

COLORADO

State Director:
Brian McNulty
Executive Director of the Special
 Education Services Unit
Colorado Department of Education
201 E. Colfax Ave.
Denver, Colo. 80203
(303)866-6694

State Plan Grant Representatives:
Nancy Sievers
Early Childhood Special Education
 Consultant
Colorado Department of Education
201 E. Colfax
Denver, Colo. 80203
(303)866-6710

David Smith
Senior Consultant, Early Childhood
Colorado Department of Education
201 E. Colfax
Denver, Colo. 80203
(303)866-6710

Elizabeth Soper
State Plan Grant Project Director
Colorado Department of Education
201 E. Colfax
Denver, Colo. 80203
(303)866-6710

Regional Resource Center Parent Representative:
Carol Wait
4511 S. Bannock
Englewood, Colo. 80110
(303)781-8368

Federally Funded Parent Training Grant:
Barbara Buswell
Parents Encouraging Parents, Inc.
1320 N. Wahsatch
Colorado Springs, Colo. 80903
(303)635-9017

State Parent Group:
Effective Parents Program (ARC)
Attn: Eula Boelke
930 Ute Ave.
Grand Junction, Colo. 81501
(303)243-4689

COMMONWEALTH OF THE NORTHERN MARIANA ISLANDS

State Plan Grant Representatives:
Bobbi Figdor
Assistant Coordinator for Early
 Childhood Programs
C.N.M.I. Department of Education
Lower Base
Saipan, Mariana Islands 96950
(670)322-9956

Cathy Yalowich
Coordinator
Handicapped Children's Resource
 Center
Division of Public Health
Saipan, Mariana Islands 96950

CONNECTICUT

State Director:
Tom Gillung
Bureau of Special Education and
 Pupil Personnel Services Chief
Connecticut Department of
 Education
P.O. Box 2219
Hartford, Conn. 06102
(203)566-3561

State Plan Grant Representatives:
Kay Halverson
Consultant for Early Childhood
 Special Education
Preschool Incentive Grant
165 Capitol Ave.
Hartford, Conn. 06106
(203)566-1961

Virginia Volk
State Plan Grant Director
State Department of Education
Box 2219
Hartford, Conn. 06145
(203)566-1961

Regional Resource Center Parent Representative:
Evan Woolacott
Combustion Engineering, Inc.
P.O. Box 500
100 Prospect Hill Road
Windsor, Conn. 06095
(203)688-1922, Ext. 3319

Federally Funded Parent Training Grant:
Nancy Prescott
Connecticut Parent Advocacy Center
c/o Mohegan Community College
Norwich, Conn. 06360
(203)886-5250

DELAWARE

State Director:
Carl Haltom
State Director
Exceptional Children/Special Programs Division
Department of Public Instruction
P.O. Box 1402
Dover, Del. 19903
(302)736-5471

State Plan Grant Representatives:
Barbara Humphreys
State Plan Grant Coordinator
Delaware Department of Public Instruction
P.O. Box 1402
Dover, Del. 19903
(302)736-4667

Deborah Ziegler
Preschool Incentive Grant Director
Lake Forest South B Elementary
Harrington, Del. 19952
(302)736-4557 or 398-8945

Regional Resource Center Parent Representative:
Nancy Horstmann
4800 Washington St. Ext.
Wilmington, Del. 19809
(302)762-1099

Federally Funded Parent Training Grant:
Patricia Gail Herbert
Parent Information Center of Delaware, Inc.
193 West Park Place
West Park Community Center
Newark, Del. 19711
(302)366-0152

DISTRICT OF COLUMBIA

State Director:
Doris Woodson
Assistant Superintendent
Division of Special Eduation and Pupil Personnel Services
D.C. Public Schools
Webster Administration Bldg.
10th and H Sts. NW
Washington, D.C. 20001
(202)724-4018

State Plan Grant Representatives:
Michelle Coleman
ECSP Program Management Specialist
Division of Special Services and Pupil Personnel Services
Webster Administrative Unit
10th and H Sts. NW
Washington, D.C. 20001
(202)724-2141

Jacquelyn Jackson
ECSP Project Coordinator
Division of Special Education and Pupil Personnel Services
Webster Administrative Unit
10th and H Sts. NW
Washington, D.C. 20001
(202)724-2141

Robbie King
Coordinator of Preschool Incentive
    Grant
Division of Special Education and
    Pupil Personnel Services
Webster Administrative Unit
10th and H Sts. NW
Washington, D.C. 20001
(202)724-4022

Maureen Thomas
Assistant to the Assistant
    Superintendent
Division of Special Education and
    Pupil Personnel Services
Webster Administrative Unit
10th and H Sts. NW
Washington, D.C. 20001
(202)724-4018

*Regional Resource Center Parent
    Representative:*
Trecy Breece
4406 S. Dakota Ave. NE
Washington, D.C. 20017
(202)576-6090 (o) or
    (202)635-7386 (h)

*Federally Funded Parent Training
    Grant:*
Marsha Parker
Parents Reaching Out Service, Inc.
D.C. General Hospital
Department of Pediatrics
West Wing, 4th Floor
1900 Massachusetts Ave. SE
Washington, D.C. 20003
(202)727-3866

FLORIDA

State Director:
Wendy Cullar
Bureau of Education for
    Exceptional Students Chief
Florida Department of Education
Knott Bldg.
Tallahassee, Fla. 32301
(904)488-1570

State Plan Grant Representatives:
Elinor Elfner
Program Development
State Department of Education
204 Knott Bldg.
Tallahassee, Fla. 32399
(904)488-5582

Patricia Hollis
State Plan Grant Coordinator
Program Specialist Supervisor
Department of Education
Bureau of Education for
    Exceptional Students
Division of Public Schools
204 Knott Bldg.
Tallahassee, Fla. 32399
(904)488-5582

*Regional Resource Center Parent
    Representatives:*
Jackie Sipple
Association for Children with
    Learning Disabilities
2881 Coral Way
Punta Gorda, Fla. 33950
(813)639-3912

Walter Schoenig
2428 Fairbanks Dr.
Clearwater, Fla. 33546
(813)536-3477

*Federally Funded Parent Training
    Grant:*
Nadine Johnson
Parent Education Network
    Florida, Inc.
2215 E. Henry Ave.
Tampa, Fla. 33610
(813)239-1179

GEORGIA

State Director:
Joan Jordan
Program for Exceptional Children
 Director
Georgia Department of Education
1970 Twin Towers East
205 Butler St.
Atlanta, Ga. 30334
(404)656-2425

State Plan Grant Representatives:
Ron Colarusso
Director of Special Education
Georgia State University
Urban Life Plaza
Atlanta, Ga. 30303
(404)658-2310

Rae Ann Redman
Consultant, Preschool Handicapped
Georgia Department of Education
1970 Twin Towers E.
Atlanta, Ga. 30334
(404)656-2426

*Regional Resource Center
 Representative:*
Joyce Long
531 Sugar Hill Dr. NW
Marietta, Ga. 30060
(404)426-3206 (o) or
 (404)422-1905 (h)

*Federally Funded Parent Training
 Grant:*
Mildred Hill
PEP Project Director
Association for Retarded Citizens
 of Georgia
1851 Ram Runway, Suite 102
College Park, Ga. 30337
(404)761-3150

State Parent Group:
Parent to Parent National
University of Georgia
850 College Station Road
Athens, Ga. 30610

GUAM

State Director:
Steve Spencer
Acting Associate Superintendent
 of Special Education
Department of Education
P.O. Box DE
Agana, Guam 96910
(671)472-8901

State Plan Grant Representative:
Faye Mata
State Plan Grant Project Director
Guam Department of Education
P.O. Box DE
Agana, Guam 96910
(671)472-8091, Ext. 379

HAWAII

State Director:
Miles Kawatachi
Special Needs Branch Director
State Department of Education
3430 Leahi Ave.
Honolulu, Hawaii 96815
(808)737-3720

State Plan Grant Representatives:
Sue Brown
State Plan Grant Project
 Coordinator
Hawaii Department of Education
Special Education Section
3430 Leahi Ave.
Honolulu, Hawaii 96815
(808)737-2564

Betty Clark Carlson
Preschool Incentive Grant
 Coordinator
Hawaii Department of Education
Special Education Section
3430 Leahi Ave.
Honolulu, Hawaii 96815
(808)737-2564

Regional Resource Center Parent Representative:
Marceline Freitas
854 Hao St.
Honolulu, Hawaii 96821
(808)471-3964

State Parent Groups:
Evalee Sinclair
Executive Director
Hawaii Association for Children and Adults with Learning Disabilities
200 N. Vinyard Blvd., Room 402
Honolulu, Hawaii 96813
(808)536-9684

Judy McGuire
Commission on the Handicapped
Old Federal Bldg.
335 Merchand St., Room 215
Honolulu, Hawaii 96813
(808)471-3964

IDAHO

State Director:
Martha Noffsinger
Special Education Supervisor
State Department of Education
650 W. State St.
Boise, Idaho 83720
(208)334-3940

State Plan Grant Representatives:
Bette Carlson
State Plan Grant Planner
Division of Community Rehabilitation
Idaho Department of Health and Welfare
450 W. State St.
Boise, Idaho 83720
(208)334-5523

Katherine Pavesic
State Plan Grant Project Manager
Bureau of Development Disabilities
Division of Community Rehabilitation
450 W. State St., 10th Floor
Boise, Idaho 83720
(208)334-5523

Regional Resource Center Parent Representative:
Sue Lundgren
Star Route 2, Box 481
Kooskia, Idaho 83539
(208)962-0062

State Parent Group:
Billie Paetel
1300 Chicadee
Boise, Idaho 83709
(208)322-8006

ILLINOIS

State Director:
Joseph Fisher
Assistant Superintendent
Illinois State Board of Education
Mail Code E-216
100 N. First St.
Springfield, Ill. 62777
(217)782-6601

State Plan Grant Representative:
Jonah Deppe
Early Intervention State Plan Coordinator
Department of Special Education Services
100 N. First
Springfield, Ill. 62777
(217)782-6601

Regional Resource Center Parent Representative:
Sally Hoerr
Illinois Alliance for Exceptional Children and Adults
515 W. Giles Lane
Peoria, Ill. 61614
(309)691-0256

Federally Funded Parent Training Grants:
Donald Moore
Designs for Change
220 S. State St.
Chicago, Ill. 60604
(312)922-0317

Charlotte DesJardins
Coordinating Council for Handicapped Children
220 S. State St., Room 212
Chicago, Ill. 60604
(312)939-3513

Advocate for Families of the Handicapped
224 W. Hickory Road
Lombard, Ill. 60148
(312)627-0603

Marjorie Lee
President
Special Education Parents Alliance
305 22nd St., Suite K-164
Glen Ellyn, Ill. 60137
(312)790-3060

INDIANA

State Director:
Gilbert Bliton
Division of Special Education Director
Indiana Department of Education
Room 229, State House
Indianapolis, Ind. 46204
(317)927-0216

State Plan Grant Representatives:
John Mefford
Chairman of the Department of Special Education
Indiana University
1700 Mishawaka Ave.
P.O. Box 7111
South Bend, Ind. 46634
(219)237-4350

Jane Schoolaert
Indiana State University
School of Education
804 Elementary/Early Education Department
Terre Haute, Ind. 47809
(812)237-2848

Regional Resource Center Parent Representative and Federally Funded Parent Training Grant:
Richard Burden
Task Force on Education of the Handicapped
812 E. Jefferson Blvd.
South Bend, Ind. 46617
(219)234-7101

State Parent Group:
Pat Koerber
Parentele
5538 N. Pennsylvania St.
Indianapolis, Ind. 46220
(317)259-1654

IOWA

State Director:
J. Frank Vance
Special Education Director
Division of Special Education
Iowa Department of Public Instruction
Grimes State Office Bldg.
Des Moines, Iowa 50319
(515)281-3176

State Plan Grant Representatives:
Joan Turner Clary
Early Childhood Special Education Program Consultant
Iowa Department of Education
Grimes State Office Bldg.
Des Moines, Iowa 50319
(515)281-3176

Peggy Cvach
State Plan Grant Consultant
Drake University
Des Moines, Iowa 50311
(515)271-3936

Regional Resource Center Parent Representative:
Deborah Samson
1721 Sixth St.
Nevada, Iowa 50201
(515)382-6082

Federally Funded Parent Training Grant:
Iowa Pilot Parents
Carla Lawson
1602 10th St. North
P.O. Box 1151
Fort Dodge, Iowa 50501
(515)576-5870

State Parent Group:
Bill Landers
Parent-Educator Partnership
4401 Sixth St. SW
Cedar Rapids, Iowa 52404
(319)399-6700 or (800)332-8488

KANSAS

State Director:
James Marshall
Director of Special Education
Kansas State Department of Education
120 E. Tenth St.
Topeka, Kan. 66612
(913)296-4945

State Plan Grant Representatives:
Suzanne Grant
State Plan Grant Coordinator
Division of Special Education
Kansas Department of Education
120 E. 10th St.
Topeka, Kan. 66612
(913)296-7453

Judy Moler
State Plan Grant Interagency Coordinator
Department of Health and Environment
Forbes Bldg., Room 740
Topeka, Kan. 66720
(913)862-9360

Regional Resource Center Parent Representative:
Marianne Ravenstein
RR #2, Box 42
Jetmore, Kan. 67854
(316)357-8361 (o) or
(316)357-6564 (h)

Federally Funded Parent Training Grant:
Patricia Gerdel
Families Together, Inc.
410 Yorkshire
Topeka, Kan. 66606
(613)273-0763

KENTUCKY

State Director:
Vivian Link
Associate Superintendent
Kentucky Department of Education
Office of Education for Exceptional Children
Room 820, Capitol Plaza Tower
Frankfort, Ky. 40601
(502)564-4970

State Plan Grant Representatives:
Betty Bright
Early Childhood Unit Director
Office of Education for Exceptional Children
Kentucky Department of Education
Room 818, Capitol Plaza Tower
Frankfort, Ky. 40601
(502)564-4970

Jeffri Brookfield-Norman
State Plan Grant Director
HDI-UAF
210A Porter Bldg.
University of Kentucky
Lexington, Ky. 40506
(606)257-8281

State Resource Directory

Maggie Chiara
Early Childhood Program
  Consultant
Office of Education for Exceptional
  Children
Kentucky Department of Education
Room 818, Capitol Plaza Tower
Frankfort, Ky. 40601
(502)564-4970

Cinda Christensen
Division of Special Services
  Director
Kentucky Department of Education
Room 822, Capital Plaza Tower
Frankfort, Ky. 40601
(502)564-4970

*Regional Resource Center Parent
  Representative:*
Gail Lincoln
Route 2, Box 214
Morehead, Ky. 40351
(606)784-7586 (o) or
  (606)783-1858 (h)

State Parent Group:
Denzil Edge
Department of Special Education
Parent Education and Resource
  Center
University of Louisville
Louisville, Ky. 40292

LOUISIANA

State Director:
Elizabeth Borel
Louisiana Department of Education
Special Educational Services
P.O. Box 94064, 9th Floor
Baton Rouge, La. 70804
(504)342-3633

State Plan Grant Representatives:
Evelyn Johnson
Interagency Coordinator State
  Plan Grant
Louisiana Department of Education
3322 Florida Blvd.
Baton Rouge, La. 70806
(504)342-6407

Ronald Lacoste
State Plan Grant Director
Section Chief Preschool Programs
3322 Florida Blvd.
Baton Rouge, La. 70806
(504)342-6407

*Regional Resource Center Parent
  Representative:*
Pat Bontempo
616 Oakwood Dr.
Gretna, La. 70053
(504)361-3377

*Federally Funded Parent Training
  Grant:*
Glennie Wray
UCP of Greater New Orleans
Harahan, La. 70183
(504)733-6851

State Parent Group:
National Federation of the Blind
  Parents Group
Dr. Joseph Feinendes
2509 Fox Creek Dr.
P.O. Box 2067
Ruston, La. 71210

MAINE

State Director:
David Noble Stockford
Division of Special Education
  Director
Maine Department of Education and
  Cultural Services
Station #23
Augusta, Maine 04333
(207)289-5953

State Plan Grant Representative:
Irving Williams
Early Childhood Consultant
Maine Department of Education
State House Section #23
Augusta, Maine 04332
(207)289-5971

Regional Resource Center Parent Representative:
Debora Tuck
11 Salmond St.
Belfast, Maine 04915
(207)338-4314

Federally Funded Parent Training Grant:
Caroline Hyde
Maine Parent Federation, Inc.
P.O. Box 2067
Augusta, Maine 04330
(207)688-4726

MARYLAND

State Director:
Martha Fields
Assistant State Superintendent
Division of Special Education
Maryland State Department of Education
200 W. Baltimore St.
Baltimore, Md. 21201
(301)659-2489

State Plan Grant Representatives:
Shelia Draper
Director, State Plan Grant, Preschool Incentive Grant
Chief, Program Development and Assistance Branch
Maryland State Department of Education
200 W. Baltimore St.
Baltimore, Md. 21201
(301)659-2495

Wanda Maynor
Assistant Director, State Plan Grant
Maryland State Department of Education
200 W. Baltimore St.
Baltimore, Md. 21201
(301)659-2495

Regional Resource Center Parent Representative:
Queen Stafford
3612 Eversley St.
Baltimore, Md. 21229
(301)566-3777 (o) or
(301)362-8571 (h)

State Parent Group:
Cory Moore
Montgomery County ARC
11600 Nebel St.
Rockville, Md. 20852
(301)984-5792

MASSACHUSETTS

State Director:
Roger Brown
Associate Commissioner
Division of Special Education
Massachusetts Department of Education
1385 Hancock St., 3rd Floor
Quincy, Mass. 02169
(617)770-7468

State Plan Grant Representatives:
Jeanne Alexandrowicz
Assistant Coordinator of Early Childhood
Division of Special Education
Massachusetts Department of Education
1385 Hancock St.
Quincy, Mass. 02169
(617)770-7478

Sharon Goldsmith
Bureau of Program Development
 Evaluation Director
Massachusetts Department of
 Education
1385 Hancock St.
Quincy, Mass. 02169
(617)770-7478

Trudy Sadeghpour
Early Childhood Special Education
 Coordinator
Division of Special Education
Massachusetts Department of
 Education
1385 Hancock St.
Quincy, Mass. 02169
(617)770-7478

Elisabeth Schaefer
Early Childhood Special Education
 Director
Division of Special Education
Massachusetts Department of
 Education
1385 Hancock St.
Quincy, Mass. 02169
(617)770-7478

*Regional Resource Center Parent
 Representative:*
Patricia Blake
P.O. Box 186
Green Harbor, Mass. 02041

*Federally Funded Parent Training
 Grant:*
Martha Ziegler
Federation for Children with Special
 Needs
312 Stuart St.
Boston, Mass 02116
(617)482-2915

State Parent Groups:
ART Project
Barbara Cutler
36 Pleasant St.
Watertown, Mass. 02172
(617)923-0797

Addie Comegy
TASH
P.O. Box 491
Wenham, Mass. 01984
(617)468-1484

VIA Inc.
Betty Hoorihan
460 Quincy Ave.
Quincy, Mass. 02169
(617)770-4000

MICHIGAN

State Director:
Edward Birch
Special Education Services Director
Michigan Department of Education
P.O. Box 30008
Lansing, Mich. 48909
(517)373-9433

State Plan Grant Representatives:
Jan Baxter
Special Education Services
 Supervisor
Michigan Department of Education
P.O. Box 30008
Lansing, Mich. 48909
(517)373-8215

Cecelia Mobley
Early Childhood Consultant
Michigan Department of Education
P.O. Box 30008
Lansing, Mich. 48909
(517)373-8483

Jim Rudolph
Special Education Evaluator
Michigan Department of Education
P.O. Box 30008
Lansing, Michigan 48909
(517)373-1830

Regional Resource Center Parent Representatives and Federally Funded Parent Training Grants:
Eileen Cassidy
Citizens Alliance to Uphold Special Education
313 W. Washington Square
Third Floor
Lansing, Mich. 48933
(517)485-4084

United Cerebral Palsy
C. Richard Heiser
7770 Second St.
Detroit, Mich. 48202
(313)871-8177

MINNESOTA

State Director:
Norena Hale
Special Education Section Manager
Department of Education
812 Capitol Square Bldg.
550 Cedar St.
St. Paul, Minn. 55101
(612)296-1793

State Plan Grant Representative:
Anita Neumann
State Plan Grant Coordinator
Minnesota Department of Education
Room 823, Capitol Square Bldg.
550 Cedar St.
St. Paul, Minn. 55101
(612)296-7032

Regional Resource Center Parent Representative:
Paula Goldberg
Codirector
PACER Center
4826 Chicago Ave. South
Minneapolis, Minn. 55417
(612)827-2966

MISSISSIPPI

State Director:
Walter Moore
Bureau of Special Services Director
State Department of Education
P.O. Box 771
Jackson, Miss. 39205
(601)359-3498

State Plan Grant Representatives:
Robert Campbell
Director
MS-UAP
Southern Station #5163
University of Southern Mississippi
Hattiesburg, Miss. 39406
(601)266-5163

Debra Montgomery
Consultant for Preschool Handicapped Programs
Bureau of Special Services
Mississippi Department of Education
P.O. Box 771
Jackson, Miss. 39205
(601)359-3488

Debbie Ruffin
Director of Division of Exceptional Student Assessment and Special Projects
Bureau of Special Services
Mississippi Department of Education
P.O. Box 771
Jackson, Miss. 39205
(601)359-3488

Becky Wilson
Coordinator of State Plan Grant
University Affiliated Programs
Southern Station #5163
Hattiesburg, Miss. 39406
(601)266-5030

State Resource Directory

Regional Resource Center Parent Representative:
Martha Lenoir
Parent Representative
1150 Arnold
Greenville, Miss. 38701
(601)332-1818

Federally Funded Parent Training Grant:
Anne Presley
President
Association of Developmental Organizations of Mississippi, Inc.
6055 Highway 18 S, Suite A
Jackson, Miss. 39209
(601)922-3210

MISSOURI

State Director:
John Heskett
Coordinator of Special Education
Department of Elementary and Secondary Education
P.O. Box 480
Jefferson City, Mo. 65102
(314)751-4909

State Plan Grant Representative:
Melodia Friedebach
State Plan Grant Project
Division of Special Education Coordinator
Department of Elementary and Secondary Education
P.O. Box 480
Jefferson City, Mo. 65101
(314)751-0706

Regional Resource Center Parent Representative:
Madeline Wendland
1018 Bedford Lane
Ballwin, Mo. 63011
(314)227-1391

MONTANA

State Director:
Gail Gray
Director of Special Education
Office of Public Instruction
State Capitol, Room 106
Helena, Mont. 59620
(406)444-4429

State Plan Grant Representatives:
Roger Bauer
State Plan Grant Coordinator
Eastern Montana College
Maternal and Child Health Care
Special Education Bldg.
1500 N. 30th St.
Billings, Mont. 59101
(406)657-2312

Michael Hagen
State Plan Grant Director
Montana Center for Handicapped Children
1500 N. 30th St.
Billings, Mont. 59101
(406)657-2312

Marilyn Pearson
EHA/B Specialist
Montana Department of Education
State Capitol
Helena, Mont. 59620
(406)444-4428

Regional Resource Center Parent Representative:
Rusty Koch
4315 Murphy Ave.
Billings, Mont. 59101
(406)248-6487

Federally Funded Parent Training Grants:
Katharin Kelker
Parents, Let's Unite for Kids
2210 Fairview Place
Billings, Mont. 59101
(406)657-2055

NEBRASKA

State Director:
Gary Sherman
Director of Special Education
Nebraska Department of Education
P.O. Box 94987
Lincoln, Neb. 68509
(402)471-2471

State Plan Grant Representative:
Jan Thelen
ECSE Consultant
Nebraska Department of Education
P.O. Box 94987
Lincoln, Neb. 68509
(402)471-2471

Regional Resource Center Parent Representative:
Michael Remus
Box 278
Osmond, Neb. 68765
(402)887-5041

State Parent Groups:
Dee Everitt
National President
Association for Retarded Citizens of the United States
4325 Meredeth
Lincoln, Neb. 68506

Brenda Sutton
Pilot Parents
3610 Dodge St.
Omaha, Neb. 68131
(402)346-5220

NEVADA

State Director:
Jane Early
Special Education Director
Nevada Department of Education
400 W. King, Capitol Complex
Carson City, Nev. 89710
(702)885-3140

State Plan Grant Representatives:
Sharon Palmer
Project Director
Nevada Department of Education
Special Education Branch
400 W. King St.
Capitol Complex
Carson City, Nev. 89710
(702)885-3140

Marilyn Walter
Grants Project Administrator
State Development Grant
Nevada State Department of Human Resources
480 Galletti Way
Sparks, Nev. 89431
(702)789-0284

Regional Resource Center Parent Representative:
Eugene Maretin
5124 Casco Way
Las Vegas, Nev. 89107
(702)386-4685 (o) or
   (702)870-8221 (h)

Federally Funded Parent Training Grant:
Vince Triggs
Director
Nevada Association for the Handicapped
P.O. Box 28458
Las Vegas, Nev. 89126
(702)870-7050

NEW HAMPSHIRE

State Director:
Robert Kennedy
Special Education Bureau Director
New Hampshire Department of Education
101 Pleasant St.
Concord, N.H. 03301
(603)271-3741

State Plan Grant Representative:
Luzanne Pierce
State Plan Grant Coordinator
Early Childhood Consultant
Special Education Bureau
State Department of Education
101 Pleasant St.
Concord, N.H. 03301
(603)271-3741

Regional Resource Center Parent Representative and Federally Funded Parent Training Grant:
Judith Raskin
Parent Information Center
P.O. Box 1422
Concord, N.H. 03301
(603)224-7005

NEW JERSEY

State Director:
Jeffrey Osowski
Division of Special Education Director
New Jersey Department of Education
P.O. Box CN 500
225 W. State St.
Trenton, N.J. 08625
(609)633-6833

State Plan Grant Representatives:
Noreen Gallagher
Manager of Programs and Services, South
New Jersey Department of Education
225 W. State St.
Trenton, N.J. 08625
(609)292-0147

Andrea Quigley
State Plan Grant Director
New Jersey Department of Education
225 W. State St.
Trenton, N.J. 08625
(609)292-0147

Regional Resource Center Parent Representative:
Esther Van Luvanee
3 Maywood Court
Fairlawn, N.J. 07410
(201)444-8882 (o) or
(201)791-2848 (h)

Federally Funded Parent Training Grants:
Mary Callahan
Involve New Jersey, Inc.
199 Pancoast Ave.
Moorestown, N.J. 08057

Jose Morales
Puerto Rican Congress of New Jersey
515 S. Broad St.
Trenton, N.J. 08611
(609)989-8888

NEW MEXICO

State Director:
Elie Gutierrez
State Director of Special Education
State Department of Education
State Educational Bldg.
Santa Fe, N.M. 87501
(505)827-6541

State Plan Grant Representatives:
Barbara Byrne-Gonzales
State Plan Grant Planner
Bureau of Developmental Disabilities
Department of Health and Environment
1190 St. Francis Dr.
Santa Fe, N.M. 87501
(505)827-6541

Louis Worley
State Plan Grant and Preschool
 Incentive Grant Coordinator
Bureau of Developmental
 Disabilities
Department of Health and
 Environment
1190 St. Francis Dr.
Santa Fe, N.M. 87501
(505)827-2575

*Regional Resource Center Parent
 Representative:*
Sharon Benson
7409 Carriveau NE
Albuquerque, N.M. 87110
(505)884-5059

*Federally Funded Parent Training
 Grants:*
James Jackson
Protection and Advocacy System
2201 San Pedro NE
Bldg. 4, Suite 140
Albuquerque, N.M. 87110
(505)888-0111

Southwest Communication
 Res., Inc.
Norman Segel
P.O. Box 788
Bernalillo, N.M. 87004
(505)867-3396

State Parent Group:
New Mexico P.R.O.
1127 University Blvd. NE
Albuquerque, N.M. 87102

NEW YORK

State Director:
Lawrence Gloeckler
Assistant Commissioner
New York State Education
 Department
Office of Education of Children
 with Handicapped Conditions
Rm. 1073, Education Bldg. Annex
Albany, N.Y. 12234
(518)474-5548

State Plan Grant Representatives:
Lawrence Gloeckler
Assistant Commissioner
New York Department of Education
Office of Education of Children
 with Handicapped Conditions
Rm. 1073, Education Bldg. Annex
Albany, N.Y. 12234
(518)474-5548

Michael Plotzker
New York Department of Education
1069 Education Bldg. Annex
Albany, N.Y. 12234
(518)474-8917

*Regional Resource Center Parent
 Representative:*
Arlene Penfield
328 Lake St.
Rouses Point, N.Y. 12979
(581)297-5331

*Federally Funded Parent Training
 Grants:*
Jane Stern
Advocates for Children of
 New York, Inc.
24-16 Bridge Plaza South
Long Island City, N.Y. 11101
(212)729-8866

Charlotte Vogelsang
Parent Network
92 Lancaster Ave.
Buffalo, N.Y. 14222
(716)882-0168

Parents Information Group
Exceptional Child
Susan Watson
#73 700 Audubon Pkwy.
Syracuse, N.Y. 13224

State Parent Groups:
New York State ARC
Marilyn Wessel, Parent Advocacy
 Coordinator
393 Delaware Ave.
Delmor, N.Y. 12054
(518)439-8311

Pat Lilac
Association for Children and Adults with Learning Disabilities
New York Chapter
155 Washington Ave.
Albany, N.Y. 12210
(518)436-4633

Esther Spindel
Association for the Learning Disabled
64-33 215th St.
Bayside, N.Y. 11364

Betty Pendler
Member, New York State Association for Retarded Children
267 W. 70th St.
New York, N.Y. 10023

NORTH CAROLINA

State Director:
E. Lowell Harris
Division for Exceptional Children Director
North Carolina State Department of Public Instruction
Room 442, Education Bldg.
116 W. Edenton
Raleigh, N.C. 27603
(919)733-3921

State Plan Grant Representatives:
Janis Dellinger
State Plan Grant Project Director
Department of Public Instruction
116 W. Edenton St.
Raleigh, N.C. 27603
(919)733-6081

Duncan Munn
Chief of Day Services
Division of MH, MR and SA
Department of Human Resources
325 N. Salisbury St.
Raleigh, N.C. 27611
(919)733-3654

Kathy Nisbet
Early Childhood Consultant
Department of Public Instruction
116 W. Edenton St.
Raleigh, N.C. 27603
(919)733-6081

Regional Resource Center Parent Representative:
Thea Monroe
2912 Debra Dr.
Raleigh, N.C. 27612
(919)782-4620

Federally Funded Parent Training Grants:
Carl Dunst
Family, Infant and Preschool Program Director
Western Carolina Center
300 Enola Road
Morganton, N.C. 28655
(704)433-2661

Connie Hawkins
Exceptional Children's Advisory Council Parent Training, Inc.
P.O. Box 16
Davidson, N.C. 29036
(704)892-1321

State Parent Group:
Parents' Educational Advocacy Center
Governor's Council for Persons with Disabilities
116 W. Jones St.
Raleigh, N.C. 27611
(919)733-9250

NORTH DAKOTA

State Director:
Gary Gronberg
Director of Special Education
Department of Public Instruction
State Capitol
Bismarck, N.D. 58505
(701)224-2277

State Plan Grant Representatives:
Brenda Oas
State Plan Grant Director
North Dakota Department of Public Instruction
State Capitol
Bismark, N.D. 58505
(701)224-2277

Mary Beth Wilson
State Plan Grant Coordinator
North Dakota Department of Public Instruction
Capitol Bldg.
Bismarck, N.D. 58505
(701)224-2277

Regional Resource Center Parent Representative:
Kathy Erickson
P.O. Box 666
Mohall, N.D. 28761
(701)268-3390

State Parent Group:
Pat Strait
1609 S. Norton
Sioux Falls, N.D. 57105
(605)336-8145

OHIO

State Director:
Frank New
Division of Special Education Director
Ohio Department of Education
933 High St.
Worthington, Ohio 43085
(614)466-2650

State Plan Grant Representatives:
Jane Wiechel
Assistant Director, Division of Educational Services
Section for Early Childhood
Ohio Department of Education
65 S. Front St.
Columbus, Ohio 43266
(614)466-0224

Linda Yoder
Educational Consultant
Division of Educational Services
Section for Early Childhood
Ohio Department of Education
65 S. Front St.
Columbus, Ohio 43266
(614)466-0224

Regional Resource Center Parent Representatives and Federally Funded Parent Training Grants:
Margaret Burley
Ohio Coalition for the Education of the Handicapped
933 High St., Suite 200H
Worthington, Ohio 43085
(614)431-1307

Thomas Murray
Executive Director
Tri-State Organized Coalition
3333 Vine St., Suite 604
Cincinnati, Ohio 45220
(513)861-2400

OKLAHOMA

State Director:
Jimmie Prickett
Special Education Section Director
State Department of Education
Room 215, Oliver Hodge Memorial Bldg.
2500 N. Lincoln
Oklahoma City, Okla. 73105
(405)521-3352

State Plan Grant Representatives:
Joanne Gordoni
Coordinator of Preschool Handicapped
Oklahoma Department of Education
2500 N. Lincoln, Suite 263
Oklahoma City, Okla. 73105
(405)521-3351

Susan Istre
State Plan Grant Coordinator
Maternal and Child Health Services
Oklahoma Department of Health
P.O. Box 53551
Oklahoma City, Okla. 73152
(405)271-4471

Regional Resource Center Parent Representative:
Cherry Taylor
4113 N.W. 59th St.
Oklahoma City, Okla. 73112
(405)946-8734

Federally Funded Parent Training Grant:
Martie Buzzard
UCP, Inc.
P.O. Box 996
Norman, Okla. 73069
(405)947-7641

State Parent Group:
Homeward Bound, Inc.
Mary Ann Becker
2415 S. Urbana
Tulsa, Okla. 74114
(918)789-7153

OREGON

State Director:
Patricia Ellis
Associate Superintendent
Special Education and Student Services Division
Oregon Department of Education
700 Pringle Pkwy. SE
Salem, Ore. 97310
(503)378-2677

State Plan Grant Representative:
Jane Toews
State Plan Grant Coordinator
Teaching Research
State System of Higher Education
345 N. Monmouth Ave.
Monmouth, Ore. 97361
(503)838-1220, Ext. 401

Regional Resource Center Parent Representative and Federally Funded Parent Training Grant:
Dr. Cheron Mayhall
Coordinator
COPE Project
999 Locust St., NE #42
Salem, Ore. 79303
(503)399-7966 or 373-7477

State Parent Groups:
William Moore
Research Professor
Oregon State System of Higher Education Teaching Research
345 N. Monmouth Ave.
Monmouth, Ore. 97361
(503)838-1220

Roz Slovic
Parents Graduation Alliance
University of Oregon
135 College of Eduation
Eugene, Ore. 97403

PENNSYLVANIA

State Director:
Gary Makuch
Bureau of Special Education Director
Pennsylvania Department of Education
333 Market St.
Harrisburg, Pa. 17126
(717)783-6913

State Plan Grant Representatives:
Jill Lichty
State Plan Grant Special Education Adviser
Bureau of Special Education
Pennsylvania Department of Education
333 Market St.
Harrisburg, Pa. 17126
(717)783-6913

Rick Price
State Plan Grant Special Education Adviser
Bureau of Special Education
Pennsylvania Department of Education
333 Market St.
Harrisburg, Pa. 17126
(717)783-6913

Regional Resource Center Parent Representative and Federally Funded Parent Training Grant:
Louise Thieme
Parent Education Network
John F. Kennedy Center
Hay Meadow Dr.
York, Pa. 17402
(717)845-9722

Federally Funded Parent Training Grant:
Christine Davis
Parents Union for Public Schools
401 N. Broad St., Room 916
Philadelphia, Pa. 19108
(215)574-0337

State Parent Group:
Ellen Siciliano
1900 Clairlon Road
West Mittlin, Pa. 15122
(412)469-2540

PUERTO RICO

State Director:
Lucila Torres Martinez
Assistant Secretary of Special Education
Department of Education
P.O. Box 759
Hato Rey, Puerto Rico 00919
(809)764-8059

State Plan Grant Representatives:
Lucila Torres Martinez
Assistant Secretary
Special Education Program
Puerto Rico Department of Education
P.O. Box 759
Hato Rey, P.R. 00919
(809)764-8059

Awilda Torres
Special Education Preschool Program Supervisor
Puerto Rico Department of Education
P.O. Box 759
Hato Rey, P.R. 00919
(809)764-8059 or 754-1771

Regional Resource Center Parent Representative and Federally Funded Parent Training Grant:
Carmen Selles Vila
Asociacion DePadres
  Pro Biene Star Ninos
  Impedides De Puerto Rico, Inc.
Box 21301
Rio Piedras, Puerto Rico 00928
(809)765-0345 (o) or
  (809)763-8485 (h)

RHODE ISLAND

State Director:
Robert Pryhoda
Special Education Program Services Unit Coordinator
Rhode Island Department of Education
Roger Williams Bldg., Room 209
22 Hayes St.
Providence, R.I. 02908
(401)277-3505

State Resource Directory

State Plan Grant Representatives:
Joan Karp
State Plan Grant Codirector
Department of Special Education
600 Mt. Pleasant Ave.
Rhode Island College
Providence, R.I. 02908
(401)456-8024

Thomas Kochanek
State Plan Grant Codirector
Department of Special Education
600 Mt. Pleasant Ave.
Rhode Island College
Providence, R.I. 02908
(401)456-8599

Regional Resource Center Parent Representative:
Nancy Husted-Jensen
Old Boston Neck Road
P.O. Box 456
Narragansett, N.Y. 02882
(401)789-9484

State Parent Group:
Parent to Parent
Joy Benson
204 Aldrich Bldg.
Rhode Island Hospital
593 Eddy St.
Providence, R.I. 02902

SOUTH CAROLINA

State Director:
Robert Black
Office of Programs for the Handicapped Director
State Department of Education
100 Executive Center Dr., A-24
Columbia, S.C. 29201
(803)758-6122

State Plan Grant Representative:
Helen Geesey
State Plan Grant Coordinator
South Carolina Department of Education
Office of Programs for the Handicapped
Santee Bldg., Suite A-24
100 Executive Center Dr.
Columbia, S.C. 29210
(803)737-8710

Regional Resource Center Parent Representative:
Betty Smith
120 Tupper Lane
Summerville, S.C. 29483
(803)871-5545

SOUTH DAKOTA

State Director:
George Levin
Section for Special Education Director
State of South Dakota Department of Education
Richard F. Neip Bldg., 3rd Floor
700 N. Illinois St.
Pierre, S.D. 57501
(605)773-3315

State Plan Grant Representative:
Paulette Levisen
Early Childhood Coordinator
South Dakota Department of Education
700 Governors Dr.
Pierre, S.D. 57501
(605)773-5239

Regional Resource Center Parent Representative:
Virginia Conlee
P.O. Box 220
Kadoka, S.D. 57543
(605)837-2211

Federally Funded Parent Training Grant:
Jan Van Veen
South Dakota Parent Connection
McKennan Hospital, Room 4509
P.O. Box 5045, 800 E. 21st St.
Sioux Falls, S.D. 57117
(605)338-3009

TENNESSEE

State Director:
Joleta Reynolds
Assistant Commissioner
Special Programs
State of Tennessee Department of Education
132 Cordell Hull Bldg.
Nashville, Tenn. 37219
(615)741-2851

State Plan Grant Representatives:
Louise Barnes
Preschool Services Specialist
Tennessee Children's Services Commission
Suite 1600
J.K. Polk Bldg., 505 Deaderick St.
Nashville, Tenn. 37219
(615)741-4505

Mary Porter
Preschool Services Coordinator
Tennessee Children's Services Commission
J.K. Polk Bldg., Suite 1600
505 Deaderick St.
Nashville, Tenn. 37212
(615)741-5274

Joleta Reynolds
Assistant Commissioner of Special Programs
Tennessee Department of Education
132 Cordell Hull Bldg.
Nashville, Tenn. 37219
(615)741-2851

Regional Resource Center Parent Representative:
Lindy Gaughn
1078 Overlook Dr.
Hendersonville, Tenn. 37075
(615)824-5287

State Parent Group:
Harriett Darryberry
EACH, Inc.
P.O. Box 121257
Nashville, Tenn. 37212
(615)298-1080

TEXAS

State Director:
Jill Gray
Special Education Programs Director
Texas Education Agency
William B. Travis Bldg., Rm. 5-120
1701 N. Congress
Austin, Texas 78701
(512)463-9414

State Plan Grant Representatives:
Donna Derkacz
State Plan Grant Coordinator
Early Childhood Intervention Program
Texas Department of Health
1110 W. 49th St.
Austin, Texas 78731
(512)465-2671

Dainey Lege
Early Childhood Preschool Incentive Grant Coordinator
Texas Education Agency
2401 Briargrove
Austin, Texas 78704
(512)463-9422

Regional Resource Center Parent Representative:
Alfonso Cervantes
150 Dexter
San Antonio, Texas 78226
(512)432-3200

Federally Funded Parent Training Grant:
Janice Foreman
ARC/TX
Early Parent Intervention
9109 Seventh St.
Orange, Texas 77630
(409)883-3324

TRUST TERRITORIES OF THE PACIFIC ISLANDS

State Directors:
Haruo "Winney" Kuraei
Federal Program Coordinator
Trust Territory of the Pacific Islands
P.O. Box 27 CHRB
Capitol Hill, Saipan CM 96950
(670)322-9870

Daniel Nielsen
Special Education Coordinator
Department of Education
Special Education Programs
Lower Base
Saipan, CM 96950
(670)322-9956

State Plan Grant Representatives:
Teresa Gamabruw
Child Find Supervisor
State Plan Grant
Yap Department of Education
Box 220
Colonia, Yap FSM 96943
(2153) (International Operator)
Routing #160 plus 691

Carol Holsinger
State Plan Grant Coordinator
Yap Department of Education
Box 220
Colonia, Yap FSM 96943
(2153) (International Operator)
Routing #160 plus 691

UTAH

State Director:
R. Elwood Pace
Coordinator of Special Education
Utah State Office of Education
250 East 500 South
Salt Lake City, Utah 84111
(801)533-5982

State Plan Grant Representatives:
Jerry Christensen
State Plan Grant Coordinator
Division of Services to the Handicapped
Utah Department of Social Services
150 W. North Temple
Salt Lake City, Utah 84145
(801)533-7146

Bonnie Morgan
Early Childhood Specialist
Utah State Office of Education
250 E. Fifth South
Salt Lake City, Utah 84111
(801)533-6040

Gary Nakao
Director DSH
State Plan Grant Codirector
Division of Services to the Handicapped
Utah Department of Social Services
150 W. North Temple, 2nd Floor
Salt Lake City, Utah 84103
(801)533-7146

Frederick White
Acting Director Family Health
State Plan Grant Codirector
Utah Department of Health
P.O. Box 16650
Salt Lake City, Utah 84116
(801)538-6161

Regional Resource Center Parent Representative:
Keith McMillan
5079 W. 3500 St.
West Valley City, Utah 84120
(801)966-1498 (o) or
  (801)969-6370 (h)

Federally Funded Parent Training Grant:
Jean Nash
Utah Coalition for Education of Handicapped Children
4984 South 300 West
Murray, Utah 84107
(801)265-9883

VERMONT

State Director:
Theodore Riggen
Executive Director
Division of Special and Compensatory Education
Vermont Department of Education
120 State St., State Office Bldg.
Montpelier, Vt. 05602
(802)828-3141

State Plan Grant Representatives:
Kristin Hawkes
Essential Early Education Consultant
Vermont Early Childhood State Plan Grant
Vermont Department of Education
Special Education Unit
120 State St.
Montpelier, Vt. 05602
(802)828-3141

Ann Marie Roy
Project Assistant
Vermont Early Childhood State Plan Grant
Vermont Department of Education
Special Education Unit
120 State St.
Montpelier, Vt. 05602
(802)828-3141

Regional Resource Center Parent Representative:
Elizabeth Milizia
239 Northgate Apts.
Burlington, Vt. 05401
(802)658-7419

Federally Funded Parent Training Grant:
Joan Sylvester
Vermont Association for Retarded Citizens
37 Champlain Mill
Winooski, Vt. 05404
(802)655-4014

VIRGIN ISLANDS

State Director:
Maureen Wynter
State Office of Special Education Director
Department of Education
P.O. Box 6640
Charlotte Amalie, St. Thomas
Virgin Islands 00801
(809)773-1095

State Plan Grant Representatives:
Dana Fredebaugh
State Plan Grant Supervisor
State Department of Education
P.O. Box 6640
St. Thomas, Virgin Islands 00801
(809)774-4399

Wanda Hamilton
State Coordinator
Early Childhood Special Education
State Department of Education
P.O. Box 6640
St. Thomas, Virgin Islands 00801
(809)774-4399

Regional Resource Center Parent Representative:
Sarah Johansen
P.O. Box 6240
Sunny Isle, Christiansted
St. Croix, Virgin Islands 00820
(809)778-1600

State Resource Directory

VIRGINIA

State Director:
N. Grant Tubbs
Administrative Director
Office of Special and Compensatory Education
Virginia Department of Education
P.O. Box 6Q
Richmond, Va. 23216
(804)225-2402

State Plan Grant Representatives:
Andrea Lazzari
Early Childhood Special Education Programs Supervisor
Virginia Department of Education
Box 6Q
Richmond, Va. 23216
(804)225-2873

Joal Read
State Plan Grant Coordinator
Virginia Department of Education
P.O. Box 6Q
Richmond, Va. 23216
(804)225-2068 or 225-2896

Regional Resource Center Parent Representative:
Jane Nott
8 Charnwood Rd.
Richmond, Va. 23229
(804)285-0907

Federally Funded Parent Training Grant:
Winifred Anderson
Project Director
Parent Education Advocacy Training Center
228 S. Pitt St., Room 300
Alexandria, Va. 22314
(703)836-2953

WASHINGTON

State Director:
Greg Kirsch
Special Education Section Director
Superintendent of Public Instruction
Old Capitol Bldg.
Olympia, Wash. 98502
(206)753-6733

State Plan Grant Representatives:
Susan Baxter
State Plan Grant Coordinator
Department of Social and Health Services
Division of Children and Family Services
Mail Stop OB-41
Olympia, Wash. 98504
(206)753-1233

Joan Gaetz
Division of Special Education Services
Old Capitol Bldg., FG-11
Olympia, Wash. 98504

Regional Resource Center Parent Representatives:
Barbara Patterson-Lehning
Parent/Community Relations
4160 86th St. SE
Mercer Island, Wash. 98040
(206)233-3396

Renee Nowak
Chairperson
Washington State Special Education Coalition
3847 48th St. SW
Seattle, Wash. 98116

Federally Funded Parent Training Grant:
Martha Gentilli
Director
Washington PAVE
1010 S. I St.
Tacoma, Wash. 98405
(206)272-7804

WEST VIRGINIA

State Director:
William Capehart
Special Education Director
W. Va. Department of Education
Bldg. #6, Room B-304
1900 Washington St. East
Charleston, W.Va. 25305
(304)348-2696

State Plan Grant Representative:
Pamela George
State Plan Grant Coordinator
W. Va. Department of Education
Room B-304, Bldg. #6
Capitol Complex
Charleston, W.Va. 25305
(304)348-2696

Regional Resource Center Parent Representative:
Helen Wilson
Early Education and Early Intervention
3309 Duley Ave., Box 4246
Parkersburg, W.Va. 26101
(304)428-8312 or 422-3151

WISCONSIN

State Director:
Victor Contrucci
Assistant State Superintendent
Division of Handicapped Children and Pupil Services
Department of Public Instruction
125 S. Webster, P.O. Box 7841
Madison, Wis. 53707
(608)266-1649

State Plan Grant Representatives:
Jenny Lange
Early Childhood Handicapped Programs Supervisor
Wisconsin Department of Public Instruction
125 S. Webster St.
P.O. Box 7841
Madison, Wis. 53707
(608)267-9172

Jim McCoy
State Plan Grant Director
Wisconsin Department of Public Instruction
125 S. Webster St.
P.O. Box 7841
Madison, Wis. 53707
(608)266-1000

Regional Resource Center Parent Representative:
Margie Gunderson-Ostroot
P.O. Box 7851
Madison, Wis. 53707
(608)266-3047

Federally Funded Parent Training Grant:
Liz Irwin
UCP of SE Wisconsin
152 W. Wisconsin Ave., #308
Milwaukee, Wis. 53203
(404)272-4500

WYOMING

State Director:
Ken Blackburn
State Department of Education
Hathaway Bldg.
2300 Capitol Ave.
Cheyenne, Wyo. 82002
(307)777-7414

State Plan Grant Representative:
Armena Taylor
Project Coordinator
State Plan Grant and Preschool Incentive Grant
University of Wyoming
P.O. Box 3114
Laramie, Wyo. 82071
(307)766-5103

Regional Resource Center Parent Representative:
Harriett Kepler
1436 Ashley
Laramie, Wyo. 82070
(307)745-9260

Bibliography

Bibliography

Alexander, Lamar, et al. "Time for Results: The Governors' 1991 Report on Education." Washington, D.C.: National Governors' Association, 1986.

Braddock, David, Richard Hemp and Ruth Howes. "Public Expenditures for the Mentally Retarded and Developmentally Disabled in the U.S." Chicago: University of Illinois Press, 1984.

Brazelton, T. Berry. "Early Intervention: What Does It Mean?" *Theory and Research in Behavioral Pediatrics*, Vol. 1. New York: Plenum Publishing Corp., 1982.

Fraas, Charlotte Jones. "Preschool Programs for the Education of Handicapped Children: Background, Issues and Federal Policy Options." Washington, D.C.: Congressional Research Service. Report No. 86-55 EPW; HV 750 A, March 17, 1986.

McLaughlin, Margaret J., Judy Smith-Davis and Philip J. Burke. *Personnel to Educate the Handicapped*. College Park, Md.: Institute for the Study of Exceptional Children and Youth, Department of Special Education, College of Education, University of Maryland, 1986.

Meisels, Samuel J., Gloria Harbin, Kathy Modigliani and Kerry Olsen. "Formulating Optimal State Early Childhood Intervention Policies." Unpublished data, December 1986.

Schonkoff, Jack P., and Penny Hauser-Cram. "Early Intervention for Disabled Infants and Their Families—A Quantitative Analysis." *Pediatrics*, 1987, in press.

Seefeldt, Carol, ed. *The Early Childhood Curriculum: A Review of Current Research*. New York City: Teachers College Press, 1987.

Smith, Barbara J., and Jacqueline A. Schakel. "Noncategorical Identification of Preschool Handicapped Children: Policy Issues and Options." *Journal of the Division for Early Childhood*, Vol. 11, No. 1, pp. 78-86. Reston, Va.: Council for Exceptional Children, 1986.

U.S. House of Representatives, Committee on Education and Labor. Report Accompanying the Education of the Handicapped Amendments of 1986, Report 99-860. Washington, D.C.: House of Representatives, 1986.

Weiner, Roberta. *P.L. 94-142: Impact on the Schools*. Alexandria, Va.: Education Research Group, Capitol Publications, 1985.

White, Karl R. "Cost Benefit Studies of Primary Prevention Programs." Family Research Coalition Report, No. 1. Chicago: Family Resource Coalition, 1985.

White, Karl. R. "The Role of Research in Formulating Public Policy About Early Intervention." Presentation to Child and Youth Research Luncheon Forum, U.S. Congress, Washington, D.C., Nov. 8, 1985.

TAKE YOUR PICK

OF THE SPECIALIZED NEWSLETTERS AND REPORTS THAT PRECISELY MEET YOUR EDUCATION INFORMATION NEEDS...

Education Daily
Eight pages daily. $429.95 per year/$245.95 for six months.
Up-to-the-minute reports on national, state and local events pertinent to top-level educators from the elementary to the postsecondary level. Includes news from Congress, the Education Department and the courts — as well as the weekly Legislative Update and the weekly supplement on available funding, **Money Alert.**

Report on Education Research
Ten pages biweekly. $169.95 per year.
News of research findings, research programs, funding and policy. Regularly covers the Education Department and the education labs and centers. Focuses on testing and evaluation, education reforms and related topics of interest to administrators and researchers.

Nation's Schools Report
Eight pages — 22 issues. $128.95 per year.
Common sense reports on what education administrators around the country are doing to pare costs and solve tangled administrative and financial problems. Includes reports on legal decisions, national news, education news, resources and more.

Education of the Handicapped
Ten pages biweekly. $180.95 per year.
The most current information available about federal legislation, regulations, programs and funding for educating handicapped children. Covers federal and state litigation under the Education for All Handicapped Children Act and other relevant laws. Looks at innovations and research in the field.

How to Evaluate Education Programs
Eight pages monthly. $119.95 per year.
Workable solutions to the most often encountered problems of education program evaluation. Covers data collecting, needs assessment and minimum competency standards. Gives fast, easy-to-understand answers to help educators master program evaluation techniques.

Report on Education of the Disadvantaged
Ten pages biweekly. $178.95 per year.
Washington news affecting Chapter 1, bilingual education, child nutrition programs, programs for migrant children and related topics of special interest. Keeps subscribers informed on program or funding changes.

School Law News
Ten pages biweekly. $177.95 per year.
Keeps school administrators and legal advisers informed of legal decisions, pending court cases and critical issues that affect schools. Covers the federal judiciary, the Supreme Court, state courts, the federal bureaucracy and developments on Capitol Hill.

Student Aid News
Ten pages biweekly. $189.95 per year.
Latest news on federal programs affecting financial aid to postsecondary students, including Guaranteed Student Loans, Pell Grants, National Direct Student Loans, Auxiliary Loans to Assist Students, Health Professions Student Loans and non-federal loan programs. Regular coverage of Congress, the Education Department and Sallie Mae.

Equal Opportunity in Higher Education
Ten pages biweekly. $171.95 per year.
Reports on all action taken in connection with claims of race, sex and handicap bias in America's postsecondary institutions. Covers federal and state court cases, legislation, regulations on affirmative action and anti-bias law compliance, and survey research results.

Tax Exempt News
Ten pages monthly. $118.95 per year.
A summary of all major news developments affecting the nonprofit community. Covers Congress, Treasury, IRS, colleges and universities, corporations that make charitable contributions, religious organizations, associations.

SPECIAL REPORTS FROM CAPITOL PUBLICATIONS' EDUCATION RESEARCH GROUP

The Child Abuse Crisis: Impact on the Schools
120 pages. $35.

Covers what states and districts are doing to detect and eliminate child abuse, the benefits and problems with screening laws and the legal responsibilities of reporting child abuse cases. Extensive statistical and resource listings.

P.L. 94-142: Impact on the Schools
365 pages. $55.

A provocative look at one of the most far-reaching pieces of federal education legislation ever, the report includes results of an exclusive survey of school administrators nationwide, complete text of the Education of the Handicapped Act and regulations, a guide to lawsuits, extensive telephone directories and more.

AIDS: Impact on the Schools
288 pages. $45.50.

Tackles the hard questions behind the AIDS-in-the-schools controversy and gives you easy-to-understand explanations of the disease itself. Extensive appendices include the text of Centers for Disease Control guidelines on AIDS in the schools, groups and associations around the country you can call for the latest facts, and an extensive glossary of AIDS-related terms.

Teen Pregnancy: Impact on the Schools
96 pages. $29.95.

Offers practical advice to school officials struggling with the many issues surrounding pregnant teens or teenage parents. Descriptions of actual programs now in use—with ways to contact their originators—are presented to help you set up similar programs in your own schools.

Education Directory: A Guide to Decisionmakers in the Federal Government, the States and Education Associations
100 pages. $45.

The most comprehensive listing available anywhere of top education administrators nationwide. Includes the Education Department and other federal agencies, chief state school officers, state education committee chairmen and more.

The Education Evaluator's Workbook: How to Assess Education Programs
Three volumes, sold separately or as a set.

The valuable workbooks offer lessons on how to conduct effective evaluations of education programs. Sample forms are included.

☐ ***Volume I:*** *The evaluation basics* $39.95
☐ ***Volume II:*** *Data collection, surveys, statistics, costs, and more* $37.95
☐ ***Volume III:*** *All about testing, and more* $36.95
   Buy any two volumes for $59.95 (a 20% savings).
   Buy the whole set for $89.95 (a 20% savings).

Education Regulations Library
Eight volumes, sold separately or as a set.

America's only customized reference library of federal education rules and laws is an eight-volume set, divided by subject and containing the full text of all regulations and laws governing education programs. A one-year subscription to **Education Regulations Update**, a monthly newsletter on regulatory changes, is included in the purchase of one or more volumes.

☐ ***Volume I: General Education Provisions*** ($59 when purchased as companion volume to any other book/$118 when purchased separately.)
☐ ***Volume II: Elementary and Secondary Education*** $195
☐ ***Volume III: Special Education*** $175
☐ ***Volume IV: Vocational Education and Job Training*** $159
☐ ***Volume V: Student Aid/Postsecondary Education*** $197
☐ ***Volume VI: Education Research*** $99
☐ ***Volume VII: Child Nutrition*** $179
☐ ***Volume VIII: Education Laws*** $229
  ☐ ***Complete Eight-Volume Set*** $969 (a 25% savings)

The Education Sourcebook: Where to Find the Materials You Need
72 pages. $19.95.

Descriptions of 293 education publications with information on who publishes them and how to order them. Grouped by subject and indexed by title and publisher.

Proven Plans for Recruiting and Retaining Students: 21 Case Studies
64 pages. $19.95.

The report offers examples of effective methods 21 postsecondary institutions have used to boost enrollment, retention rates, public image and funding.

Also available from the Education Research Group:

A complete document retrieval service. For a master list of available documents, or for personalized document retrieval services, contact the Education Research Group's document research specialist at (703) 683-4100.

Education Research Group, Capitol Publications, Inc., 1101 King Street, P.O. Box 1453, Alexandria, VA 22313-2053

Use This Coupon To Order Additional Copies Of
FROM BIRTH TO FIVE:
SERVING THE YOUNGEST HANDICAPPED CHILDREN

☐ **YES**, I need to know what I can do to comply with new provisions of the Education of the Handicapped Act. Please rush me _____ copy(ies) of **FROM BIRTH TO FIVE: SERVING THE YOUNGEST HANDICAPPED CHILDREN** at _____ per copy.

Name_____

Organization_____

Address_____

City_____ State_____ ZIP_____

☐ Check enclosed (payable to Capitol Publications, Inc.)
☐ Bill me/my organization
   Purchase order number _____
☐ Charge ☐ VISA ☐ MasterCard
          ☐ American Express

Account number _____ Expiration date _____

Signature (required for billing and credit orders) _____

Telephone _____

For fastest service, call
TOLL-FREE 1-800-327-7204
M-F, 9-5 EST. In Virginia, call collect (703) 739-6500.

Education Research Group, Capitol Publications, Inc.
1101 King Street, P.O. Box 1453, Alexandria, VA 22313-2053

The most sweeping changes in education for handicapped children since P.L. 94-142.

P.L. 99-457 The Next Step Forward for Handicapped Children

A new video training program has been developed by The Council for Exceptional Children to help educators, advocates, and social service agency workers learn about the new federal legislation passed in October 1986. These materials describe how services for handicapped children from birth through 5 have been strengthened and how interagency support will help enhance service delivery.

This media package is most helpful in providing an overview to professionals responsible for implementing the new programs. It is designed for inservice training in schools and social service agencies.

Package Contents:
- 23-minute VHS casette.
- Masters for 21 overhead transparencies.
- Copies of the *Act* and the *Report*.
- 4 fact sheets.
- Users Guide.

Prepared by Joseph Ballard, Frederick J. Weintraub, and Kathy Zantal-Wiener, Department of Governmental Relations.
Stock Number 317. Price: $147.00

Q & A Also Available

P.L. 94-142, Section 504, and P.L. 99-457— Understanding What They Are and What They Are Not

This newly revised question-and-answer document reflects the latest changes in legislation affecting the education of handicapped children. 1987, Stock No. 196. Price: 1-9 copies $4.00 each; 10 copies, $20.00; 50 copies, $50.00.

For further information call or write:
The Council for Exceptional Children
Publication Sales Dept. 9945H
1920 Association Drive
Reston, Virginia 22091-1589
703/620-3660